THE EARLY HANOVERIAN AGE 1714-1760

ALSO BY A.F. SCOTT

MEANING AND STYLE
POETRY AND APPRECIATION
MODERN ESSAYS (three series)
TOPICS AND OPINIONS (three series)
THE SPOKEN WORD (two series)
SPEAKING OF THE FAMOUS
VITAL THEMES TODAY
THE CRAFT OF PROSE
CURRENT LITERARY TERMS
(A Dictionary of their Origin and Use)
ANGLO-BENGALI SCHOOL FINAL ENGLISH
COMPOSITION AND TRANSLATION
(with Professor Dharanimohan Mukherjee)
NEW HORIZONS, in ten books (with N.K. Aggarwala)
(Macmillan)
ENGLISH COMPOSITION (in four books)
POEMS FOR PLEASURE (in three books)
PLAIN ENGLISH (in five books)
THE POET'S CRAFT
Cambridge University Press
CLOSE READINGS
(Heinemann)
WHO'S WHO IN CHAUCER
(Hamish Hamilton)
WITCH, SPIRIT, DEVIL

EVERY ONE A WITNESS
The Georgian Age
The Stuart Age
The Plantagenet Age
The Tudor Age
The Norman Age
The Roman Age
The Saxon Age

THE EARLY HANOVERIAN AGE 1714-1760
Commentaries of an Era

A.F. Scott

CROOM HELM LONDON

© 1980 Scott and Finlay Ltd
Croom Helm Ltd, 2-10 St John's Road, London SW11

British Library Cataloguing in Publication Data

Scott, Arthur Finlay
    The early Hanoverian age, 1714-1760.
    1. England — Civilization — 18th century
    I. Title
    942.07   DA485
    ISBN 0—7099—O145—3

To ALAN and DOREEN YOUNG

Printed in Great Britain by Biddles Ltd, Guildford, Surrey

Contents

Illustrations

The author and publishers acknowledge with thanks permission to reproduce the illustrations listed below.

Acknowledgements

The author and publishers are grateful to the authorities named for permission to use copyright material. Furthermore, the publishers have tried to trace the owners of all copyright material, and apologise for any omissions. Should these be made known to us, proper acknowledgements will be made in future editions.

9

The Triumph of the Family of George I in the Painted Hall at Greenwich. The stern-faced, elderly lady behind the King is his mother, Sophia, a granddaughter of James I, through whom he inherited the throne. Above him, to his right, is his daughter, Sophia Dorothea, and his daughter-in-law, Caroline of Anspach (holding a mirror). To his left is his grandson Frederick, father of George III. On the left are his other grandchildren. Above is the figure of justice, with St Paul's in the background – Mural by R.N.C. Greenwich.

The first forty years of the Eighteenth Century, the reign of Anne and the rule of Walpole, constitute an age of transition, during which the feuds and ideals of the Stuart era, lately a lava flood scouring the land with devastating heat, were being channelled and congealed into fixed, durable Hanoverian forms. In this way the age of Marlborough and Bolingbroke, of Swift and Defoe, was the meeting-point of two epochs. It is only in the years that followed (1740-1780) that we find a generation of men wholly characteristic of the Eighteenth Century ethos, a society with a mental outlook of its own, self-poised, self-judged, and self-approved, freed from the disturbing passions of the past, and not yet troubled with anxieties about a very different future which was soon to be brought upon the scene by the Industrial and the French Revolutions. The gods mercifully gave mankind this little moment of peace between the religious fanaticisms of the past and the fanaticisms of class and race that were speedily to arise and dominate time to come. In England it was an age of aristocracy and liberty; of the rule of law and the absence of reform; of individual initiative and institutional decay; of Latitudinarianism above and Wesleyanism below; of the growth of humanitarian and philanthropic feeling and endeavour; of creative vigour in all the trades and arts that serve and adorn the life of man.

It is a 'classical' age, that is to say an age of unchallenged assumptions, when the philosophers of the street, such as Dr. Johnson, have ample leisure to moralize on the human scene, in the happy belief that the state of society and the modes of thought to which they are accustomed are not mere passing aspects of an ever-shifting kaleidoscope, but permanent habitations, the final outcome of reason and experience — G.M. Trevelyan.

1 Royalty

George I (1714-1727)

George I was lazy and inactive even in his pleasures, which therefore were lowly sensual. He was coolly intrepid and indolently benevolent. He was diffident of his own parts, which made him speak little in public and prefer in his own social, which were his favourite hours, the company of wags and buffoons. Even his mistress, the Duchess of Kendal, with whom he passed most of his time and who held all influence over him, was little better than an idiot. Importunity alone could make him act, and then only to get rid of it. His views and affections were singly confined to the narrow compass of his Electorate. England was too big for him. . . . The King loved pleasure, and was not delicate in his choice of it. No woman came amiss of him, if they were very willing and very fat . . . the standard of His Majesty's taste made all those ladies who aspired to his favour, and who were near the statutable size, strain and swell themselves like the frogs in the fable to rival the bulk and dignity of the ox. Some succeeded, and others burst — Lord Chesterfield, *Miscellaneous Works*, 1777.

George I, from a painting by Sir Godfrey Kneller.
'Wha the deil hae we goten for a King — But a wee wee German lairdie?' — *Jacobite Relics of Scotland*.
   Ragnhild Hatton's book shows him to be the most competant and politically imaginative of our Hanoverian kings.

13

George II (1727-1760)

But after this last journey Hanover had so completed the conquest of his affections, that there was nothing English ever commended in his presence that he did not always show, or pretend to show, was surpassed by something of the kind in Germany. No English or even French cook could dress a dinner; no English confectioner set out a dessert; no English player could act; no English coachman could drive, or English jockey ride, nor were any English horses fit to be drove or fit to be ridden; no Englishman knew how to come into a room, nor any Englishwoman how to dress herself; nor were there any diversions in England, public or private; nor any man or woman in England whose conversations was to be borne – the one, as he said, talking of nothing but their dull politics, and the others of nothing but their ugly clothes. Whereas at Hanover all these things were in the utmost perfection; the men were patterns of politeness, bravery, and gallantry; the women of beauty, wit, and entertainment; his troops there were the bravest in the world, his counsellors the wisest, his manufacturers the most ingenious, his subjects the happiest; and at Hanover, in short, plenty reigned, magnificence resided, art flourished, diversions abounded, riches flowed, and everything was in the utmost perfection that contributes to make a prince great or a people blessed.

. . . In truth he hated the English, looked upon them all as king-killers and republicans, grudged them their riches as well as their liberty, thought them all overpaid, and said to Lady Sundon one day as she was waiting at dinner, just after he returned from Germany, that he was forced to distribute his favours here very differently from the manner in which he bestowed them at Hanover; that there he rewarded people for doing their duty and serving him well, but that here he was obliged to enrich people for being rascals, and buy them not to cut his throat – Lord Hervey, *Some Material Towards Memoirs of the Reign of King George II*.

The Monotonous Daily Round

'In 1760 George II was seventy-seven years of age, and the weary, never changing round of court life, to which he kept himself and his court so meticulously, had gone on for thirty-three years.' *Bemoaning this monotony Lord Hervey wrote to a friend:*

I will not trouble you with any account of our occupations at Hampton Court. No mill-horse ever went in a more constant track, or a more unchanging circle; so that, by the assistance of an almanack for the day of the week, and a watch for the hour of the day, you may inform yourself fully, without any other intelligence but your memory, of every transaction within the verge of the Court. Walking, chaises, levees, and audiences fill the morning. At night the King plays at commerce and back-gammon . . . The Duke of Grafton takes his nightly opiate of lottery, and sleeps as usual between the Princesses Amelia and Caroline. Lord Grantham strolls from one room to another (as Dryden says), like some discontented ghost that oft appears, and is forbid to speak; and stirs himself about as people stir a fire, not with any design but in hopes to make it burn brisker. At last the King gets up; the pool finishes; and everybody has their dismission, and thus the evening and the morning make the day.

George II, from a painting by Thomas Hudson.
'Everything in his composition was little, and he had all the weaknesses of a little mind, without any of the virtues or even the vices of a great one' — the Earl of Chesterfield.

15

Queen Caroline of Anspach, wife of George II, 'the power behind the throne. Dignified and unassuming, charming in her natural distinction, and in her easy and pleasant conversation, she discusses the most important problems with accurate knowledge, in a judicious manner such as is rarely found in women' — Duvenvoidre, a Dutch diplomat. Bust by John Ichael Rysbrack.

The Funeral of George II

Horace Walpole attended the funeral, and describes the solemn occasion with a light, diverting touch.

Do you know I had the curiosity to go to the burying t'other night; it is absolutely a noble sight. The Prince's chamber, hung with purple, and a quantity of silver lamps, the coffin under a canopy of purple velvet, and six vast chandeliers of silver on high stands, had a very good effect . . . The procession, through a line of footguards, every seventh man bearing a torch, the horse-guards lining the outside, their officers with drawn sabres and crape sashes on horseback, the drums muffled, the fifes, bells tolling, and minute guns — all this was very solemn . . . But . . . when we came to the chapel of Henry the Seventh, all solemnity and decorum ceased; no order was observed, people sat or stood where they could or would; the yeoman of the guard were crying out for help, oppressed by the immense weight of the coffin; the Bishop read sadly, and blundered in the prayers; the fine chapter, *Man that is born of a woman*, was chanted, not read; and the anthem, besides being immeasurably tedious, would have served as well for a nuptial. The real serious part was the figure of the Duke of Cumberland, heightened by a thousand melancholy circumstances . . . He bore it all with a firm and unaffected countenance. This grave scene was fully contrasted by the burlesque figure of the Duke of Newcastle. He fell into a fit of crying the moment he came into the chapel, and flung himself back in a stall, the Archbishop hovering over him with a smelling-bottle; but in two minutes his curiosity got the better of his hypocrisy, and he ran about the chapel with his glass to spy who was or was not there, spying with one hand, and mopping his eyes with the other. Then returned the fear of catching cold; and the Duke of Cumberland, who was sinking with heat, felt himself weighed down, and turning round, found it was the Duke of Newcastle standing upon his train, to avoid the chill of the marble.

2 London

The Organised Child Market

'In great demand amongst the army of beggars were young children whose simulated misery and poverty was always good for a coin.'

Having one day rambled into the Heart of the good parish of St Giles' in the Fields, I stood staring and gaping about, like the mayor of a country corporation in the Court of Requests, till at length I came to a place call'd the Infant Office where young children stand at livery and are let out by the day to the town mendicants. The first scene that presented was a little villain of about four years old who, upon my asking him some questions, told me that his father had been a house-carpenter in Dublin where he broke his neck by a fall from a scaffold, in repairing a cellar window, and died about seven years before he was born. A woman of about seventy would needs hire a baby that was sucking at the breast, and another, who had a complexion as sallow as a Portuguese sailor, must forsooth be accommodated with a child as fair as a smock-fac'd parson. One woman hired no less than four for the day; two she pack'd up behind her like a Scotch pedlar's budget, the third was to run by her side bawling out for victuals, and the fourth she held in her arms, like a tuneable instrument to be set to musick, when she came in the view of any seemingly well-dispos'd people. An ancient matron, who had the super-intendency of the office, held forth in her arms a pretty poppet of about a year old, telling them there was a sweet innocent picture, a moving countenance, that would not fail making a sergeant-at-law feel for his half-pence, and would extort charity even from a divine. A beggar woman, who was vastly in arrear for the lett of children, was refus'd any longer credit till she paid off the old score, and made no more to do but threw an old ragged riding-hood over her shoulders, cursing them for a parcel of unchristian old bitches in forcing her to tell the town ten thousand lyes, by saying she had three poor infants sick at home.

Every one being suited according to their circumstances and convenience, it was not altogether an unpleasing sight to behold this little auxiliary army off to lay a great Protestant city and its suburbs under contribution – from a contemporary pamphlet, *A Trip Through the Town.*

Noisy Turbulence of London

London is a world by itself; we daily discover in it more new centuries and surprising singularities than in all the universe besides. There are among the Londoners so many nations differing in manners, customs, and religions, that the inhabitants themselves don't know a quarter of 'em. Imagine, then, what an Indian would think of such a motley herd of people, and what a diverting amusement it would be to him to imagine with a traveller's eye all the remarkable things of this mighty city. A whimsy takes me in the head to carry this stranger all over the town with me: no doubt but his odd and fantastical ideas will furnish me with variety, and perhaps with diversion . . .

I will therefore suppose this Indian of mine dropped perpendicularly from the clouds, to find himself all of a sudden in the midst of this prodigious and noisy city, where repose and silence dare scarce show their heads in the darkest night. At first dash the confused clamours near Temple Bar stun him, fright him, and make him giddy.

He sees an infinite number of different machines, all in violent motion, with some riding on the top, some within, others behind, and Jehu on the coach-box, whirling towards some dignified villain who has got an estate by cheating the public. He lolls at full stretch within, with half a dozen brawny, bulk-begotten footmen behind . . .

Some carry, others are carried. 'Make way there,' says a gouty-legged chair-man, that is carrying a punk of quality to a morning's exercise; or a Bartholomew baby-beau, newly launched out of a chocolate house, with his pockets as empty as his brains. 'Make room there,' says another fellow, driving a wheelbarrow of nuts that spoil the lungs of the city 'prentices and make them wheeze over their mistresses as bad as the phlegmatic cuckolds, their masters, do when called to family duty. One draws, the other drives. 'Stand up there, you blind dog,' says a carman, 'will you have the cart squeeze your guts out?' One tinker knocks, another bawls, 'Have you brass-pot, iron-pot, kettle, skillet or frying-pan to mend?' Another son of a whore yelps louder than Homer's stentor, 'Two a groat, and four for sixpence, mackerel.' One draws his mouth up to his ears and howls out, 'Buy my flounders,' and is followed by an old burly drab that screams out the sale of her 'maids' and her 'soul' at the same instant.

Here a sooty chimney-sweeper takes the wall of a grave alderman, and a broom-man jostles the parish parson. There a fat greasy porter runs a trunk full-butt upon you, while another salutes your antlers with a basket of eggs and butter. 'Turn out there, you country putt,' says a bully with a sword two yards long jarring at his heels, and throws him into the kennel. By and by comes a christening, with the reader screwing up his mouth to deliver the service *à la mode de Paris*, and afterwards talks immoderately nice and dull with the gossips, the midwife strutting in the front with young original sin as fine as fippence; followed with the vocal music of 'Kitchen-stuff ha' you maids,' and a damned trumpeter calling in the rabble to see a calf with six legs and a top-knot — Tom Brown, from *Amusements, Serious and Comical Calculated for the Meridian of London*, 1700.

Bedlam: A Public Diversion of the Time

It was the Hospital of St Mary of Bethlehem, converted to an asylum for the insane in 1547. People went there to tease the inmates. Admission was one penny. Bedlam was also a popular place of business for the whores of London.

Bedlam is a pleasant place, that it is, and abounds with amusements. The first is the building so stately a fabric for persons wholly insensible of the beauty and the use of it; the outside is a perfect mockery to the inside, and admits of two amusing queries, whether the persons that order the building of it, or those that inhabit it, were the maddest? But what need I wonder at that, since the whole is but one entire amusement? Some were preaching, and others in full cry a-hunting; some were praying, others cursing and swearing; some were dancing, others groaning; some singing, others crying; and all in perfect confusion. A sad representation of the greater chimerical world! Only in this there's no whoring, cheating, or fleecing, unless after the Platonic mode, in thought, for want of action. However, any gentleman that is disposed for a touch of the times, may take his choice for the price of one penny, which is Cerberus's fee at the entry; or any lady that has got the *prurigo copulandi* has a spark at her service to be found walking here at any time of the day. Is your wife or your daughter mad, for something that shall be nameless? Send 'em hither to be made sober. Or has one relation, male or female, that's over-bashful? Let not either him or her despair of a cure, for here are guests enough to teach 'em to part with their modesty.

Here are persons confined that having no money nor friends, and but a small stock of confidence run mad for want of preferment; a poet that, for want of wit and sense, ran mad for want of victuals; and a hard-favoured citizen's wife, that lost her wits because her husband had so little as to let her know that he kept a handsome mistress. In this apartment is a common lawyer pleading; in another a civilian sighing; a third encloses a Jacobite, ranting against the Revolution; and a fourth, a morose, melancholy Whig, bemoaning his want of an office and complaining against abuses at court, and mismanagements. A fifth has a comical sort of a fellow, laughing at his physician, Doctor Tyson, for his great skill in taciturnity; and a sixth a Cantabrigian organist for its tenant, that had left sonnet and madrigal for philosophy, and had lost his senses while he was in pursuit of knowledge — Tom Brown, from *Amusements III, London*, 1700.

Lotteries in London

State lotteries were popular in England at this time. A writer in the Spectator Papers *gives some information:*

I know a well-meaning man that is very well pleased to risk his good fortune upon the number 1711, because it is the year of our Lord. I have been told of a certain zealous dissenter, who, being a great enemy to Popery, and believing that bad men are the most fortunate in this world, will lay two to one on the number 666 against any other number; because, he says, it is the number of the beast.

The Coffee-House

Macaulay says, 'The coffee-house was the Londoner's home, and those who wished to find a gentleman commonly asked, not whether he lived in Fleet Street or Chancery Lane, but whether he frequented the Grecian *or the* Rainbow.' *The* Rainbow *was probably the very first of London coffee-houses.*

I am lodged in the street called Pall-Mall, the ordinary residence of all strangers, because of its vicinity to the King's Palace, the Park, the Parliament House, the theatres, and the chocolate and coffee-houses, where the best company frequent. If you would know our manner of living it is thus: — we rise by nine, and those that frequent great men's levees find entertainment at them till eleven; or, as in Holland, go to tea-tables. About twelve the *beau-monde* [fashionable society] assembles in various chocolate and coffee-houses, the best of which are the Cocoa Tree [a chocolate house at end of Pall-Mall, frequented by Tories] and White's Chocolate-houses, St. James's [another Whig house]; the Smyrna [a house offering elevated conservation and also bohea (tea) and snuff] and the British Coffee-houses; and all these so near one another, that in less than an hour you see the company of them all. We are carried to these places in chairs (sedans), which are here very cheap, a guinea a week or a shilling per hour; and your chairmen serve you for porters to run on errands, as your gondoliers do at Venice.

If it be fine weather we take a turn in the park till two, when we go to dinner; and if it be dirty, you are entertained at picket or basset [card games] at White's, or you may talk politics at the Smyrna and St. James's. I must not forget to tell you that the parties have their different places, where, however, a stranger is always well received; but a Whig will no more go to the Cocoa Tree or Ozinda's, than a Tory will be seen at the Coffee-house of St. James's.

The Scots generally go to the British, and a mixture of all sorts to the Smyrna. There are other little coffee-houses much frequented in this neighbourhood — Youngman's, for officers; Oldman's, for stock-jobbers, paymasters, and courtiers; and Littleman's, for sharpers. I never was so confounded in my life as when I entered into this last; I saw two or three tables full at faro [gambling card game], heard the box and dice rattling in the room above stairs, and was surrounded by a set of sharp faces that I was afraid would have devoured me with their eyes. I was glad to drop two or three half-crowns at faro to get off with a clear skin, and was overjoyed I was so got rid of them.

At two we generally go to dinner. Ordinaries [public meal provided at a fixed time and price at a tavern] are not so common here as abroad, yet the French have set up two or three pretty good ones for the conveniency of foreigners, in Suffolk-street, where one is tolerably well served; but the general way here is to make a party at the coffee-house to go dine at the tavern, where we sit till six, then we go to the play.

After the play, the best company generally go to Tom's and Willis's coffee-houses [kept by waiters who had saved money for the purpose] near adjoining, where there is playing at 'Picket' and the best of conversation till midnight. Here you will see blue and green ribands and stars sitting familiarly with private gentlemen, and talking with the same freedom as if they had left their quality and degrees of distance at home; and a stranger tastes with pleasure the universal liberty of speech of the English nation. Or if you like rather the company of ladies, there are assemblies at most people at quality's houses. And in all the coffee-houses you have not only the foreign prints, but several English ones, with the foreign occurrences, besides papers of morality and party disputes – John Macky, *Journey through England*, 1724.

Cleanliness Indeed

In 1726 C. de Saussure describes what he saw in London:

The amount of water English people employ is inconceivable, especially for the cleaning of their houses. Though they are not slaves to cleanliness, like the Dutch, still they are very remarkable for this virtue. Not a week passes by but well kept houses are washed twice in the seven days and that from top to bottom; and even every morning most kitchens, staircases and entrances are scrubbed. All furniture, and especially all kitchen utensils, are kept with the greatest cleanliness. Even the large hammers and the locks on the door are rubbed and shine brightly.

Lord Mayor's Day

Rowdy London paid little respect to courtesy. One delight was to bait foreigners.

The Lord Mayor's day is a great holiday in the City. The populace on that great day is particularly insolent and rowdy, turning into lawless freedom the great liberty it enjoys. At these times it is almost dangerous for an honest man, and particularly for a foreigner, if at all well dressed, to walk in the streets, for he runs a great risk of being insulted by the vulgar populace, which is the most cursed breed in existence. He is sure of not only being jeered at and being bespattered with mud, but as likely as not dead dogs and cats will be thrown at him, for the mob makes a provision beforehand of these playthings, so that they may amuse themselves with them on the great day — César de Saussure, *Letter to Swiss friend*, 1727.

London Streets

London has neither troops, patrol nor any sort of regular watch and it is guarded during the night only by old men chosen from the dregs of the people, who have no other arms but a lanthorn and a pole, who patrol the streets, crying the hour every time the clock strikes, who proclaim good or bad weather in the morning, who come to awake those who have any journey to perform, and whom it is customary with young rakes to beat and use ill, when they come reeling from the taverns where they have spent the night.

The English themselves acknowledge that London swarms with pickpockets as daring as they are subtle and cunning. Though I was always in the streets, and in the midst of multitudes whom chance threw in my way, and though I never took any care of my pocket, I had no reason to complain of suffering by their subtlety, which I encouraged by my carelessness. After taking a walk one evening in the avenue to Chelsea Hospital, I sat down upon a bench where I fell asleep with a book in my hand; upon waking, I found myself surrounded with old soldiers, one of whom told me in French that I had run a great risk in giving way to sleep in that manner. I knew, answered I, that I was surrounded with military men and brave fellows. What hazard could I run in such company? Having said this, I gave the Frenchman a shilling for his information — César de Saussure, *A Foreign View of England in the Reigns of George I and George II*, 1725-9.

Earthquakes in London

Seventeen-fifty is the most memorable year of English earthquakes. On 8 February a shock was felt, followed exactly a month afterwards by a second and severer one, 'when the bells of the church clock struck against chiming hammers.'
Walpole tells of the catastrophe in a letter to Sir Horace Mann:

My text is not literally true; but, as far as earthquakes go towards lowering the price of wonderful commodities, to be sure we are over-stocked. We have had a second, much more violent than the first; and you must not be surprised if, by next post, you hear of a burning mountain springing up in Smithfield. In the night between Wednesday and Thursday last, the earth had a shivering fit between one and two; but so slight that, if no more had followed, I don't believe it would have been noticed. I had been awake, and had scarce dozed again – on a sudden I felt my bolster lift my head. I thought somebody was getting from under my bed, but soon found it was a strong earthquake, that lasted nearly half a minute, with a violent vibration and great roaring. I got up and found people running into the streets, but saw no mischief done. There has been some; two old houses flung down, several chim-neys, and much earthenware. The bells rang in several houses. Admiral Knowles, who has lived long in Jamaica, and felt seven there, says this was more violent than any of them. The wise say, that if we have not rain soon, we shall certainly have more. Several people are going out of town, for it has nowhere reached above ten miles from London: they say they are not frightened, but that it is such fine weather, 'Lord, one can't help going into the country!' The only visible effect it has had was in the Ridotto, at which, being the following morning, there were but 400 people. A parson who came into White's the morning after earth-quake the first, and heard bets laid on whether it was an earthquake or the blowing up of powder mills, went away exceedingly scandalised, and said, 'I protest they are such an impious set of people, that I believe, if the last trumpet was to sound, they would bet puppet-show against judgment!' The excitement grew intense: following the example of Bishops Secker and Sherlock, the clergy showered down sermons and exhortations, and a country quack sold pills 'as good against an earthquake.' A crazy Lifeguardsman predicted a third and more fatal earthquake at the end of four weeks after the second; and a frantic terror prevailed as the time drew near.

'On the evening preceding the 5th of April, the roads out of London were crowded with vehicles, spite of an advertisement in the papers threatening the publication "of an exact list of all the nobility and gentry who have left or shall leave this place through fear of another earthquake." "Earthquake gowns" – warm gowns to wear while sitting out of doors all night – were in great request with women. Many people sat in coaches all night in Hyde Park, passing away the time with the aid of cards and candles;' and Walpole asks his correspondent, 'What will you think of Lady Catherine Pelham, Lady Frances Arundel,

25

and Lord and Lady Galway, who go this evening to an inn ten miles out of town, where they are to play brag till four o'clock in the morning, and then come back, I suppose, to look for the bones of their husbands and families under the rubbish?' The prophet of all this was a trooper of Lord Delawar's, who was sent to Bedlam.

The second shock having happened exactly a month after the former, it was believed there would be a third in another month, which was to swallow up London; and Walpole advised several who were going to keep their next earthquake in the country, to take the bark for it, as they were so periodic. Dick Leveson and Mr Rigby, who had supped and stayed late at Bedford House, one night, knocked at several doors, and in a watchman's voice cried, 'Past four o'clock, and a dreadful earthquake!'

Dangerous Districts

Whoever considers the Cities of London and Westminster with the late vast increases of their suburbs the great irregularity of their buildings, the immense number of lanes, alleys, courts and bye-places, must think that they had been intended for the very purpose of concealment, they could not have been better contrived. Upon such a view the whole appears as a vast wood or forest in which the thief may harbour with as great security as wild beasts do in the deserts of Arabia and Africa — Henry Fielding, *Inquiry into the Cause of the Late Increase of Robbers*, 1751.

Nuisances of the Time

An Englishman sets out the nuisances of the time, 1760.

He would wish to see the butchers' boys, who gallop through the streets of London, punished for so doing, or at least their horses seized for the use of the poor of the parish in which they offend; for though a poor man's life may not be worth preserving, his limbs may be of use to him while he crawls upon earth.

Brewers starting their butts in the day-time, he considers as an intolerable nuisance.

Ruinous houses ought to be pulled down, because they may as well tumble upon the head of an alderman as upon that of a cobbler.

A regulation in Smithfield market, he thinks, ought to take place, because a mad ox may as well gore the lady of a knight-baronet as a poor oyster wench.

That cheesemongers should not set out their butter and cheese so near the edge of their shop-windows, nor put their firkins in the pathways, by which many a good coat and silk gown may be spoiled; as by advertising in the papers his shop will be sufficiently known, without carrying home the shop-bill upon our clothes.

Ladders, pieces of timber, etc, should by no means be suffered to be carried upon men's shoulders within the posts of this city, because, by a sudden stop, they may as well poke out the eye of a rich man as that of a poor one.

Chair-men, as they are a kind of human nags, ought to amble withoutside the posts as well as other brutes.

It is needless for ladies of a certain cast to patrol the streets at noonday with a bundle in one hand, as they carry an evident sign of their profession in their eye.

Barbers and chimney-sweepers have no right by charter to rub against a person well-dressed, and then offer him satisfaction by single combat.

3 Towns, Buildings and Gardens

Stourbridge Fair at Cambridge

To attend this Fair, and the prodigious conflux of people which come
to it, there are sometimes no less than fifty hackney coaches, which
come from London, and ply night and morning to carry the people to
and from Cambridge; for there the gross of them lodge; nay, which is
still more strange, there are wherries brought from London on waggons,
to ply upon the little river Cam, and to row people up and down from
the town and from the Fair. . . .

It is not to be wondered at if the town of Cambridge cannot receive
or entertain the numbers of people that come to this Fair; not Cambridge only but all the towns round are full; nay, the very barns and
stables are turned into inns, and made as fit as they can to lodge the
meaner sort of people; As for the people in the Fair, they all universally
eat, drink, and sleep in their booths and tents; and the said booths are
so intermingled with taverns, coffee-houses, drinking-houses, eating-
houses, cooks' shops, etc., and all in tents, too, and so many butchers
and higglers from all the neighbouring counties come into the Fair
every morning with beef, mutton, fowls, butter, bread, cheese, eggs
and such things, and go with them from tent to tent, from door to door,
that there's no want of any provisions of any kind, either dressed or
undressed. In a word, the Fair is like a well-governed city — Daniel
Defoe, *A Tour Through the Whole Island of Great Britain*, 1722.

Houses Altered to Meet the New Style

The Duchess of Marlborough writing to the Duchess of Bedford.

June 17th, 1734
I have been this day at Bedford House, though I could not go out of
my coach. You know I always liked it. But now it is so much mended
by the new wing and the doing it with stucco that I am sure there is not

28

Blenheim Palace, near Bladon and Woodstock in Oxfordshire, designed
and built for the Duke of Marlborough by John Vanbrugh in 1715.
*'Erected at the Publick Expense in Commemoration of the Victory at
Blenheim, and settled on the Great Duke of Marlborough and his
Descendants for ever.'*

so good a house anywhere in the world. There is more convenience than
in any house that I ever saw; and the two courts that are placed on each
side of the house for the stables and offices are better placed than even
I saw any in the town or in the country. And in short, everything is
done, with good sense; which I am sure no architect now living is
capable of doing...

June 21st 1734

I was very sincere in what I said of Bedford House, which is the name
I think it should now go by. It is altogether the most noble and agreeable thing that ever I saw in my life but there is yet one thing that I
think would amend it, and I should think cannot be a great expense.
I did not name it in my last because Mr Smith told me that it could not
be altered because it would darken some windows. But upon reflection
I think there must be some other reason for it, that I believe is not a
good one. What I mean is the stairs in the first court, which, though
they were Inigo Jones's doing, certainly are not handsome and look too

much pinched in the middle. And I do think now the house is so extremely fine and large with the two wings it would be much handsomer if it was made with a flight of stairs like those at Marlborough House with large half paces; and a great deal of the stone would serve again, either on that side or the garden front. And I do not see how it could darken anything, unless the room under the hall; which as I remember was only designed for chairmen and footmen to wait in. Which use does not want a great deal of light. . . .

The Gothic, Chinese and Other Fancies

> Some cry up Gunnersbury,
> For Sion some declare,
> And some say that with Chiswick House
> No villa can compare:
> But ask the beaux of Middlesex
> Who know the country well,
> If Strawberry Hill, if Strawberry Hill
> Don't bear away the bell.

The Earl of Bath, *The Gentleman's Magazine*, April 1756.

Building Practice of the Mid-Eighteenth Century

We see many very beautiful pieces of workmanship in red brick; and to name one, the front of the green-house in Kensington-Gardens will be sure to attract every eye that has the least curiosity: but this should not tempt the judicious architect to admit them in the front walls of the building.

In the first place, the colour is itself fiery and disagreeable to the eye; it is troublesome to look upon it; and, in summer, it has an appearance of heat that is very disagreeable: for this reason it is most improper in the country, though the oftenest used there, from the difficulty of getting grey.

But a farther consideration is, that in the fronts of most buildings of any expence there is more or less stonework: now . . . there is something harsh in the transition from the red brick to stone, and it seems

Holkham Hall, Norfolk. Designed by William Kent, 1734, helped by Lord Burlington in the Palladian style, for the owner Thomas Coke, Earl of Leicester. Coke was at the time Britain's greatest farmer.

altogether unnatural; in the other, the grey stocks come so near the colour of stone that the change is less violent, and they sort better together.

For this reason also the grey stocks are to be judged best coloured when they have least of the yellow cast; for the nearer they come to the colour of stone, when they are to be used together with it, always the better.

Where there is no stone work there generally is wood, and this being painted white, as is commonly the practice, has a yet worse effect with red brick than the stone work; the transition is more sudden in this than the other: but, on the other hand, in the mixture of grey bricks and white paint, the colour of the brick being soft, there is no violent change — Isaac Ware, *A Complete Body of Architecture*, 1756.

The English Landscape Garden

But here nature, though too much herself, was infinitely better than where every step savoured of art, and every tree bled from the sheers. We now despice these; and have between the two extremes of absolute wild nature and precise art, hit upon a very just method: we need only pursue the same principles, and we shall bring it to perfection. What we propose now in Gardens is to collect the beauties of nature; to separate them from those rude views in which her blemishes are seen, and to bring them nearer to the eye; to dispose them in the most pleasing order and create an universal harmony among them: that every thing may be free, and nothing savage; that the eye may be regaled with the collected beauties of the vegetable world, brought together from the remotest regions, without that formality which was once understood to constitute the character of a garden: and that the farther views be open to the horizon. Thus the eye delights itself at its own choice with the charms of the particular object, or the vast assemblage of the whole: philosophick mind is detained upon the construction of a flower; while the free fancy of another turn is charmed with hill and lawn, and slope and precipice; and sees in one great view beyond the limits of the bounding walls, all those charms that can arise from wood and water, burnt heaths and waving forests.

Our gardens are thus more regular than those of our ancestors; in effect more extensive; and throughout agreeable: everything pleasing is thrown open; everything disgustful is shut out, nor do we perceive the

Strawberry Hill: the Twickenham villa bought by Horace Walpole in 1747. Extensions that he made are shown on the right.

art, while we enjoy its effects: the sunk wall prevents your knowing where the garden terminates; and the very screen from unpleasing objects seems planted only for its natural beauty — Isaac Ware, *A Complete Body of Architecture*, 1756.

Social Life in a Sussex Village

1757 Feb. 22 (*Wednesday*). About four p.m. I walked down to Whyly. We played at bragg [a game at cards] the first part of the even. After ten we went to supper on four boiled chicken, four boiled ducks, minced veal, sausages, cold roast goose, chicken pasty, and ham. Our company, Mr. and Mrs. Porter, Mr. and Mrs. Coates, Mrs. Atkens, Mrs. Hicks, Mr. Piper and wife, Joseph Fuller and wife, Dame Durrant, myself and wife, and Mr. French's family. After supper our behaviour was far from that of serious, harmless mirth; it was downright obstreperous, mixed with a great deal of folly and stupidity. Our diversion was dancing or jumping about, without a violin or any music, singing of foolish healths, and drinking all the time as fast as it could be poured down; and the parson of the parish was one among the mixed multitude. If conscience declares right from wrong, as doubtless it sometimes does, mine is one that I may say is soon offended; for, I must say, I am always very uneasy at such behaviour, thinking it not like the behaviour of the primitive Christians, which I imagine was most in conformity to our Saviour's gospel. Nor would I be thought to be either a cynic or a stoic, but let social improving discourse pass round the company. About three o'clock, finding myself to have about as much liquor as would do me good, I slipt away unobserved, leaving my wife to make my excuse. Though I was very far from sober, I came home, thank God, very safe and well, without even tumbling; and Mr. French's servant brought my wife home at ten minutes past five — Thomas Turner, *Diary*, 1754-65.

4 Family

Marriage Customs

When those of a middling condition have a mind to be so extravagant as to marry in public (which very rarely happens) they invite a number of friends and relations. Everyone puts on new clothes and dresses finer than ordinary; the men lead the women, they get into coaches and so go in procession and are married in full day at church. After feasting and dancing and having made merry that day and the next, they take a trip into the country and there divert themselves very pleasantly. These are extraordinary weddings. The ordinary ones, as I said before, are generally incognito. The bridegroom, that is to say the husband that is to be, and the bride, who is the wife that is to be, conducted by their father and mother, or by those that serve them in their room, and accompanied among others, by two bride-men and two bride-maids, go early in the morning with a licence in their pocket, and call up Mr. Curate and his clerk, tell him their business, are married with a low voice and the doors shut; tip the minister a guinea and the clerk a crown, steal softly out, one one way, and t'other another, either on foot or in coaches, go different ways to some tavern at a distance from their lodgings or to the house of some trusty friend, there have a good dinner and return home at night as quietly as lambs. If the drums and fiddles have notice of it they will be sure to be with them by daybreak, making a horrible racket till they have got the pence. And when bed-time is come, the bride-men pull off the bride's garters, which she had before untied that they might hang down. This done and the garters being fastened to the hats of the gallants, the bride-maids carry the bride into the bed-chamber, where they undress her and lay her in bed. (They must throw away and lose all the pins. Woe be to the bride if a single one is left about her, for then nothing will go right. Woe also to the bride-maids if they keep one of them, for they will not be married before Whitsuntide.)

35

The bridegroom, who by the help of his friends is undressed in some other room, comes in his nightgown, as soon as possible, to his spouse, who is surrounded by mother, aunt, sister, and friends, and without any further ceremony gets into bed. Some of the women run away, others remain, and the moment afterwards they are all got together again. The bride-men take the bride's stockings, and the bride-maids the bride-groom's. Both sit down at the bed's feet and fling the stockings over their heads, endeavouring to direct them so as they they may fall upon the married couple. If the man's stockings, thrown by the maid, fall upon the bridegroom's head, it is a sign she will quickly be married herself, and the same prognostic holds good of the woman's stockings, thrown by the man. Oftentimes these young people engage with one another upon the success of the stockings, though they themselves look upon it to be nothing but sport. While some amuse themselves agreeably with these little follies, others are preparing a good posset, which is a kind of caudle, a potion made up of milk, wine, yolks of eggs, sugar, cinnamon, nutmeg, etc. This they present to the young couple, who swallow it down as fast as they can, to get rid of so troublesome company. The bridegroom prays, scolds, entreats them to be gone and the bride says ne'er a word, but thinks the more. If they obstinately continue to retard the accomplishment of their wishes, the bridegroom jumps up in his shirt, which frightens the women and puts them to flight; the men follow them and the bridegroom returns to the bride.

They never fail to bring them another sack-posset next morning. The young woman, more gay and more contented than ever she was in her life, puts on her finest clothes (for she was married only in a mob), the dear husband does the same, and so do the young guests; they laugh, they dance, they make merry, and these pleasures continue a longer or shorter time, according to the several circumstances of things – M. Misson, *Memoirs and Observations*, 1719.

The Training of a Family in Scotland

Those that could afoard governesses for their Children had them; but all they could learn them was to read English ill, and plain work. The chief thing required was to hear them repeat Psalms and long catechisms, in which they were employed an hour or more every day, and almost the whole day on Sunday. If there was no governess to perform this work, it was done by the chaplan, of which there was one in every family. No attention was given to what we call accomplishments. Reading and writing well or even spelling was never thought off. Musick, drawing, or French were seldom taught the girls. They were allow'd to run about and amuse themselves in the way they choiced even to the age of women, at which time they were generally sent to Edinr. for a winter or two, to lairn to dress themselves and to dance and to see a little of the world. The world was only to be seen at Church, at marriages, Burials, and Baptisams. These were the only public places where the Ladys went in full dress, and as they walked the street they were seen by every body; but it was the fashion when in undress allwise to be masked. When in the country their employment was in color'd work, beds, Tapestry, and other pieces of furniture; immitations of fruit and flowers, with very little taste. If they read any it was either books of devotion or long Romances, and sometimes both. They never eat a full meal at Table; this was thought very undelicat, but they took care to have something before diner, that they might behave with propriety in company. From the account given by old people that lived in this time, we have reason to believe there was as little care taken of the young men as of the women; excepting those that were intended for lairned professions, who got a regular education throw schools and coledges. But the generallity of our Country gentlemen, and even our Noblemen, were contented with the instruction given by the Chaplin to their young men — Elizabeth Mure, *Some Observations of the Change of Manners in My Own Time*, 1700-1790.

FOOD AND DRINK

Spirits

Spirits openly sold in 6,187 houses and shops in London, 1725.

And although this number is exceeding great . . . [being in some parishes every tenth house, in others every seventh, and in one of the largest, every fifth house) the committee believe it to be very far short of the true number, there being many who sell . . . even in the streets and highways, some on bulks set up for that purpose, and others in wheelbarrows, and many more who sell privately in garrets, sellars, backrooms and other places. . . . The committee observe with deep concern the strong inclination of the inferior sort of people to these destructive liquors, and yet, as if that were not sufficient, all arts are used to tempt and invite them. All chandlers, many tobacconists, and such who sell fruit or herbs in stalls and wheelbarrows sell geneva, and many inferior tradesmen begin now to keep it in their shops for their customers, whereby it is scarce possible for soldiers, seamen, servants, or others of their rank, to go anywhere without being drawn in either by those who sell it or by their acquaintance, whom they meet with in the street, who generally begin by inviting them to a dram. ... In the hamlet of Bethnal Green above forty weavers sell it. And if we may judge what will happen in other workhouses now erecting, by what has already happened in that of St Giles in the Fields, we have reason to fear that the violent fondness and desire of this liquor, which unaccountably possesses all our poor, may prevent in great measure the good effects proposed by them ... it appearing by the returns from the Holborn division that notwithstanding all the care that has been taken, Geneva is clandestinely brought in among the poor there, and that they will suffer any punishment ... rather than live without it, though they cannot avoid seeing its fatal effects by the death of those among them who had drunk most freely of all – *Order Book*, Middlesex Sessions.

A Four-Penny Dinner

Living at Edinburgh continued still [in 1742] to be wonderfully cheap, as there were ordinaries for young gentlemen, at fourpence a-head for a very good dinner of broth and beef, and a roast and potatoes every day, with fish three or four times a-week, and all the small-beer that was called for till the cloth was removed – Alexander Carlyle, *Autobiography*.

Tea Drinking in Nottingham

The People here are not without their Tea, Coffee, and Chocolate, especially the first, the Use of which is spread to that Degree, that not only the Gentry and Wealthy Traders drink it constantly, but almost every Seamer, Sizer and Winder, will have her Tea and will enjoy herself over it in a Morning, not forgetting their snuff, a pinch or two of which they never fail of regaling their Nostrils with between every dish; and even a Common Washerwoman thinks she has not had a proper Breakfast without Tea and hot buttered white Bread ... being the other Day at a Grocers, I could not forbear looking earnestly and with some Degree of Indignation at a ragged and greasy Creature, who came into the Shop with two Children following her in as dismal a Plight as the Mother, asking for a Pennyworth of Tea and a Halfpennyworth of Sugar, which when she was served with, she told the Shop-keeper: Mr. N. I do not know how it is with me, but I can assure you I would not desire to live, if I was to be debarred from drinking every Day a little Tea – Charles Deering, *Nottingham Vetus and Nova*, 1751.

Gin

Wretches are often brought before me, charged with theft and robbery, whom I am forced to confine before they are in a condition to be examined; and when they have afterwards become sober, I have plainly perceived from the state of the case, that the Gin alone was the cause of the transgression, and have been sometimes sorry that I was obliged to commit them to prison. . . . Gin is the principal sustenance (if it may be so called) of more than an hundred thousand people in this metropolis. Many of these wretches there are, who swallow pints of this poison within the twenty four hours; the dreadful effects of which I have the misfortune every day to see, and to smell too – Henry Fielding, *An Inquiry into the Causes of the Late Increase of Robbers*, 1751.

DRESS

Dress in Scotland

The 1727 is as far back as I can remember. At that time there was little bread in Scotland; Manefactorys brought to no perfection, either in linnen or woolen. Every woman made her web of wove linnen, and bleched it herself; it never rose higher than 2 shillings the yeard, and with this cloth was every body cloathed. The young gentlemen, who at this time were growing more delicat, got their cloth from Holland for shirts; but the old was satisfied with necks and sleeves of the fine, which were put on loose above the country cloth. I remember in the 30 or 31 [1730 or 1731] of a ball where it was agreed that the company should be dress'd in nothing but what was manufactur'd in the country. My sisters were as well dressed as any, and their gowns were strip'd linen at 2s. and 6d. per yard. Their heads and ruffles were of Paisley

39

muslings, at 4 and sixpence, with four peny edging from Hamilton; all of them the finest that could be had. A few years after this, wevers were brought over from Holland, and manefactorys for linen established in the West. The dress of the ladys were nearly as expencive as at present, tho not so often renewed. At the time I mention houps were worn constantly 4 yards and a half wide, which required much silk to cover them; and gould and silver was much used for trimming, never less than three rows round the peticot; so that tho the silk was slight the price was increased by the triming. Then the heads were all dress'd in laces from Flanders; no blonds nor courssedging used; the price of those was high, but two sute would serve for life; they were not re-newed but at marriage or some great event. Who could not afoard those wore fringes of thread — Elizabeth Mure, *Some Observations of the Change of Manners in My Own Time, 1700-1790.*

Improvement in Dress

Among all classes, as great an improvement has taken place with respect to dress as in almost any other article. Before the year 1760 none of the poor, or only a small proportion of them, wore stockings. Even in the houses of gentlemen of high rank, the maidservants seldom used them in the earlier part of the day, while employed in servile work. The celebrated Charles Townshend used to give a ludicrous description of his being received by a 'female porter' without stockings or shoes, when he paid his respects to Lord President Craigie in the Lawnmarket, Edinburgh, in 1758 or 1759, and also of the practice, at the time general in the country, of the women treading their dirty linen, instead of washing it with their hands.

The dress both of men and women alike in the middle and higher ranks exhibited by turns the extremes of gaudy ostentation and disgus-ting slovenliness. Not only the hats, but the body clothes of gentlemen in full dress, were fringed with gold or silver lace. The hats were all then cocked. (Velvet caps, however, were worn by many of the gentlemen, and leather caps frequently by the farmers). At an early period of my life a few of the country gentlemen of more advanced age wore swords when in full dress, and I knew aged persons who remembered swords being held as an indispensable article of fashionable costume. The dis-continuance of this practice may be considered as in moral view an important improvement on the fashions of our fathers. On the occasion of sudden quarrels, especially in drunken brawls, the ready command

Colonel Charles Ingram and his Children, by P. Mercier, 1741. The son
is in a coat with 'mariner' cuffs (slit vertically and buttoned); breeches
buckled over the stockings. The daughter in a back-fastening gown,
apron with bib, pinner on her head. The father in laced coat and
waistcoat and roll-up stockings.

of a dangerous weapon was unfortunately the frequent cause of blood-shed. . . . Ladies when visiting or receiving company, wore silk gowns, or riding habits with gold or gilded buttons and fringes. A silk plaid wrapped loosely about the head and body was the prevailing fashion at church. Patches on the face formed a part of the full dress of ladies, particularly of those further advanced in life. The fashion was beginning to wear out in my early life. I have not seen an instance of it for the last fifty or fifty-five years; but I recollect many persons who followed it before that time, and have seen the patch-boxes, which once made a part of the furniture of every ladies' dressing closet.

The undress of both sexes was often coarse and slovenly beyond any example even among the lower orders in modern days. Gentlemen used to walk about all the morning in greasy night caps and dirty night-gowns (dressing-gowns) or thread-bare coats. The elder ladies wore large linen caps called *toys*, encroaching on the face, and tied under the chin, with worsted shortgowns and aprons. The word toy is probably derived from the French *toque*, the hood worn by women of mean condition in France – Thomas Somerville, *My Own Life and Times*, 1741-1814.

FURNISHING

Enamelled Salt-Glazed Stoneware

> To please the noble dame, the courtly Squire
> Produced a Tea Pot made in Staffordshire.
> So Venus looked, and with such longing eyes
> When Paris first produced the golden prize.
> 'Such works as this', she cries, 'can England do?
> It equals Dresden, and excels St. Cloud.'

Sir Charles Hanbury-Williams, Isabella, 1740.

Porcelain Figures

Jellies, biscuits, sugar-plumbs, and creams have long given way to harle-quins, gondoliers, Turks, Chinese, and shepherdesses of Saxon China. But these, unconnected and only seeming to wander among groves of curled paper, and silk flowers, were soon discovered to be insipid and

Mrs Birch and Daughter, by Joseph Highmore, 1745. The mother in
a wrapping gown with edge-to-edge closure. The daughter's coiffure
shows a *tête de mouton* and on the head a pompon.

unmeaning. By degrees whole meadows of cattle, of the same brittle materials, spread themselves over the whole table; cottages rose in sugar, and temples in barley-sugar; pigmy Neptunes in cars of cockleshells, triumphed over oceans of looking glass or seas of silver tissue, and at length the whole system of Ovid's metamorphosis succeeded to all the transformations which Chloe and other great professors had introduced into the science of hieroglyphic eating. Confectioners found their trade moulder away, while toymen and china-shops were the only fashionable purveyors of the last stage of polite entertainments. Women of the first quality came home from Chenevix's laden with dolls and babies, not for their children, but their housekeeper. At last even these puerile puppet-shows are sinking into disuse, and more manly ways of concluding our repasts are stablished. Gigantic figures succeed to pigmies; and if the present taste continues, Rysbrack, and other neglected statuaries, who might have adorned Grecian salons, though not Grecian desserts, may come into vogue – Horace Walpole, *The World*, 8 February 1753.

Mr B. finds Pamela writing. An illustration by Joseph Highmore in *Pamela* by Samual Richardson, 1740.

The picture well illustrates the style of furnishing to be found in the middle-class home.

Neatness of Workmanship

. . . tho' the moderns have not made many additions to the art of building, with respect to mere beauty of ornament, yet it must be confess'd, they have carried simplicity, convenience, and neatness of workmanship, to a very great degree of perfection, particularly in England; where plain good sense hath preferr'd these more necessary parts of beauty, which everybody can understand, to that richness of taste which is so much to be seen in other countries, and so often substituted in their room – William Hogarth, *The Analysis of Beauty*, 1753.

Cabinet-Making

Of all the Arts which are either improved or ornamented by Architecture, that of CABINET-MAKING is not only the most useful and ornamental, but capable of receiving as a great assistance from it as any whatever. I have therefore prefixed to the following designs a short explanation of the five orders. Without an acquaintance with this science, and some knowledge of the rules of Perspective, the Cabinet-Maker cannot make the designs of his work intelligible, nor shew, in a little compass, the whole conduct and effect of the piece. These, therefore, ought to be carefully studied by every one who would excel in this branch, since they are the very soul and basis of his art – Thomas Chippendale, *The Gentleman and Cabinet Maker's Director*, 1754.

Chinese Idolatry

The simple and sublime have lost all influence, almost everywhere, all is Chinese or Gothic. Every chair in an apartment, the frames of glasses, and tables must be Chinese: the walls covered with Chinese paper fill'd with figures which resemble nothing of God's creation, and which a prudent nation would prohibit for the sake of pregnant women . . . Nay, so excessive is the love of Chinese architecture become, that at present foxhunters would be sorry to break a leg in pursuing their sport in leaping any gate that was not made in the eastern taste of little bits of wood standing in all directions.

The gothic, too, has its advocates; you see a hundred houses built with porches in that taste, such as are belonging to many chapels; not to mention that rooms are stuccoed in this taste, with all the minute unmeaning carvings, which are found in the most Gothic chapels of a thousand years standing — John Shebbeare, *B. Angeloni, Letters on the English Nation*, 1755.

Tapestry Designs

Found on English chairs and fire-screens, mid-eighteenth century.

3 patterns for screens with a Flowerpot and a Parrot. . . .
1 ditto with 3 beautiful India Birds, another with Apollo and Daphne. . . .
A pattern for a screen or chair with the fable of the Stork and the Fox. . . .
Similar items for the Wolf and the Stork, the Fox and the Grapes, the Monkey and the Cat, the Stag and the Lamb. . . .
11 large chair seats with curious Baskets of Flowers. . . .
A large and magnificent State-chair, the back with beautiful Fowls and the seat a Landskip.

Catalogue of Sale, 1755.

Interior Decoration

The decoration of the inside of rooms may be reduced to three kinds; first those in which the wall itself is properly finished with elegance; that is where the materials of its last covering are of the finest kind, and it is wrought into ornaments plain or uncovered; secondly where the walls are covered with wainscot; and thirdly where they are hung; this last article comprehending paper, silk, tapestry and every other decoration of this kind. For a noble hall nothing is so well as stucco; for a parlour wainscot seems properest; and for the apartment of a lady, hangings — Isaac Ware, *A Complete Body of Architecture*, 1756.

Receipt for Painting Rooms

For painting your Rooms lay them over with white Lead and oil, tinctured with a little blue Blake and see that it be thin laid over so that it may drown the Knots, afterwards mix your white Lead with turpentine Varnish half of each, when it is fully dryed and lay it over, and you may depend on't you'll have a clear gloss. Blue Blake is one penny per ounce. Buy one quarter of a pound, when I speak of the first colouring lay it thin over, is meant the colour must be mixed thin with the oil for the first painting. Buy one quarter of an ounce of Prussian blue which will be two shill: sterl. which will serve all your rooms. Brushes, one at one shilling sterl. one at 8 ds. and another at 6 ds. which is all.

Make your white Lead the thickness of cream for the painting, and mix it with Blue blake. 2nd. Painting, mix your colour of the same thickness above mentioned, but put one half turpentine Varnish with the Colour after it is grinded, and tincture it with a little Prussian Blue
— Elizabeth Raper, *The Receipt Book*, 1756-1770.

5 Education

Remarks upon the University of Cambridge

After the coach had set me down, and I had taken a fair leave of my fellow-travellers, I walked about, to take a more complete survey of the town and University. The buildings in many parts of the town were so little and so low, that they looked more like huts for pygmies, than houses for men; and their shopkeepers seemed to me to be so well-sized to their inhabitations, that they appeared like so many monkeys, in their diminutive shops, mimicking the trade of London. Amongst the rest of the pomps and vanities of this wicked Corporation, there is one very famous inn, distinguished by the sign of the Devil's Lapdog in Petty-Cury; here I went to refresh myself with a glass or two of Canary; where I found an old grizzly curmudgeon, corniferously wedded to a plump, young, brisk, black, beautiful, good landlady; who, I afterwards heard, had so great a kindness for the University, that she had rather see two or three gownmen come into her house than a cuckoldy crew of aldermen in all their pontificalibusses: and indeed, I had reason to believe there was no love lost, for the scholars crept in as fast, and as slyly, for either a kiss, a kind look, or a cup of comfort; as hogs into an orchard after a high wind, or flies into pig sauce, for the sake of the sugar; I liked my pretty hostess so wonderfully well, and was so greatly delighted with the pleasant conversation I met with in the house, that I determined with myself to make this my place of residence, during my continuance in the town; so bespeaking a bed, I afterwards took a walk in order to view the University, of which I shall proceed to give you a sober and concise description.

The colleges stand outside the town, which, in plain terms, is a corporation of ignorance, hemmed round with arts and sciences, a nest of fools, that dwell on the superfluities of the learned, an ungrateful soil where the seeds of generosity are daily scattered, but produce nothing in return, but with wicked weed of unthankfulness and ingratitude. Of learned societies there are in all sixteen, twelve colleges, and four halls, the most magnificent of which, being that of Trinity, whose spacious quadrangle, and commodious library, remain without comparison. The scholars of this foundation are distinctly habited in purple gowns; the rest of the University wearing black, agree in one and the same mode. The next piece of building more particularly remarkable is King's College Chapel, founded by Henry the Sixth, and is greatly famed by all men of judgment for its admirable architecture, much after the manner of Henry the Seventh's chapel at Westminster, if not finer and larger. The rest of the colleges, except St. John's (which has been beautified and enlarged of late years) wear the faces of great antiquity, and though they are not so fine as those which have had the advantage of a modern improvement, yet the rust of the aged walls, and obsoleteness of their structure, procure veneration from all spectators, and seemed to me more noble in their ancient uniformity, than others disagreeable enlarged with additional novelties. In short, the colleges are so splendid, the government so regular, the orders so strict, the ceremonies so decorous and the preferments so honourable, that in all Europe, it is not excelled by any university, except Oxford — Edward Ward, from *A Step to Stir-Bitch-Fair, with Remarks upon the University of Cambridge*, 1700.

George I's Gift of the Bishop of Ely's Library to Cambridge University

Our royal master saw, with heedful eyes,
The wants of his two universities:
Troops he to Oxford sent, as knowing why
That learned body wanted loyalty:
But books to Cambridge gave, as well discerning
That that right loyal body wanted learning.

Letter from School

From William Cotesworth at Sedbergh to his father, 7 April 1716.

Honoured Father,

We arrived here on Wednesday night. Our Landlady is a very neat woman, and as far as we have tried, does very well by us. We have always 2 Dishes of meat to dinner and there are three sorts of Bread set

upon the table, and we have liberty to choose of which we will. As for our breakfasts, we have butter and bread and cheese, and as much milk as we desire, and if we be hungry betwixt meals she bids us call for what we want. We have a little room entire to ourselves where we have shelves for our books, and pins for our cloths, and there's a room almost as large as the Hall [at their home] which we have liberty to walk in. Mr. Saunders [the Headmaster] seems to be a very civil man and calls every day to see us. We gave him everyone a Guinea and my Uncle [according to the custom of the School] gave the Usher half as much . . .   Your Dutyful son,
William Cotesworth

Charity Schools

It is manifest that in a free nation where slaves are not allowed, the surest wealth consists in a multitude of laborious poor; for besides that they are the never failing nursery of fleets and armies, without them there could be no enjoyment and no product of any country could be valuable. To make society happy and people easy under the meanest circumstances, it is requisite that great numbers of them should be ignorant as well as poor. Knowledge both enlarges and multiplies our desires, and the fewer things a man wishes for, the more easily his necessities may be supplied.

The welfare and felicity therefore of every state and kingdom, require that the knowledge of the working poor should be confined within the verge of their occupations, and never extended (as to things visible) beyond what relates to their calling. The more a shepherd, a ploughman, or any other peasant knows of the world, and the things that are foreign to his labour or employment, the less fit he'll be to go through the fatigues and hardships of it with cheerfulness and content.

Reading, writing, and arithmetic are very necessary to those whose business require such qualifications, but where people's livelihood has no dependence on those arts, they are very pernicious to the poor, who are forced to get their daily bread by their daily labour. Few children make any progress at school, but at the same time they are capable of being employed in some business or other, so that every hour those of poor people spend at their books is so much time lost to society. Going to school in comparison to working is idleness, and the longer boys continue in this easy sort of life, the more unfit they'll be when grown up for downright labour, both as to strength and inclination. Men who are to remain and end their days in a laborious, tiresome, and painful station of life, the sooner they are put upon it at first, the more patiently they'll submit to it for ever after. Hard labour and the coarsest diet is a proper punishment to several kinds of malefactors, but to impose either on those that have not been brought up to both is the greatest cruelty, when there is no crime that you can charge them with. . . . Those who spent a great part of their youth in learning to read, write, and cypher expect, and not unjustly, to be employed where those qualifications may be of use to them; the generality of them will look upon downright labour with the utmost contempt. A man who has had some education, may follow husbandry by choice, and may be diligent at the dirtiest and most laborious work; but then the concern must be his own, and avarice, the care of a family, or some other pressing motive must put him upon it, but he won't make a good hireling and serve a farmer for a pitiful reward, at least he is not so fit for it as a day labourer that has always been employed about the plough and dung-cart, and remembers not that ever he has lived otherwise — B. Mandeville, *An Essay on Charity and Charity Schools*, 1723.

A charity school in the eighteenth century. From a contemporary engraving. 'The object of the schools from the beginning was to preserve children from vagrancy and to fit them for some sort of regular work.' From an engraving by J. Allen.

51

Schoolboy Diet at Christ's Hospital

The children are dieted in the following manner: They have every morning for their breakfast bread and beer, at half an hour past six in the morning in the summer time, and at half an hour past seven in the winter. On Sundays they have boiled beef and broth for their dinners, and for their suppers leg and shoulders of mutton. On Tuesdays and Thursdays they have the same dinners as on Sundays, that is, boiled beef and broth; on the other days no flesh meat, but on Mondays milk-porridge, on Wednesdays furmity [wheat boiled in milk], on Fridays old pease and pottage, on Saturdays water-gruel. They have roast beef about twelve days in the year, by the kindness of several benefactors, who have left, some £3 some 50s *per annum*, for that end. Their supper is bread and cheese, or butter for those that cannot eat cheese; only Wednesdays and Fridays they have pudding-pies for supper.

The diet of these children seems to be exceeding mean and sparing; and I have heard some of their friends say, that it would not be easy for them to subsist upon it without their assistance. However, it is observed they are very healthful; that out of eleven or twelve hundred, there are scarce ever found twelve in the sick ward; and that in one year, when there were upwards of eleven hundred in this hospital, there were not more than fifteen of them died. Besides, their living in this thrifty parsimonious manner, makes them better capable of shifting for themselves when they come out into the world — Don Manoel Gonzales, *Voyage to Great Britain, c.* 1730.

From the Rules of Worcester Cathedral Choir School

Of the Schole

That the Schole be visited by the Dean or Subdean and prebendaries at least twice in the year on June 23 if not a Sunday otherwise the day before and on the first day of Audit and some publick Exercises be performed at those times.

That the children be examined as to their Books, Exercises and Catechism and that such orders as shall be judged proper for the government of the School be given at those times.

That all the children of the School do constantly bring Common Prayer Books with them to Church, and that one or more monitors be appointed by the Masters to note such as come without Books.

That the children do at no time play or loiter in any part of the Church, and that they never play in the Cloysters in School hours otherwise to be severly chastised by the Master.

That no King's Scholar be suffered to continue in the School as such a fifth year if he be fifteen years of age compleat, Except he be a Chorister of the Church or be designed for the University.

That every child before he be admitted a King's Scholar to bring to the Master a Certificate of his age signed by the Minister and one of the Churchwardens of the parish where he was born.

That no children who are maintained at an Alehouse be received into the School.

That Parents shall freely suffer their children to be chastised for their faults and forebear coming to the School on such occasions that the Masters may not be interrupted or discouraged in the performance of their Duty. But if they have any just Occasion for Complaint that it be made to the Dean, Subdean or Senr Prebendary present, and that the children of such parents as will not observe this Rule to be turned out of the School.

That none of the Children do presume to come to any person to ask a Play without the Master's leave and that no play be given untill he have first been advised with — *c.* 1730.

School: University: Grand Tour

To Eaton sent, o'er every Form you leapt,
No studious Eves, no toilsome Mattins kept,
Thence Christ's Quadrangle took you for its own;
Had Alma Mater e'er so true a Son!
Half seven Years spent in Billiards, Cards and Tippling,
And growing every day a lovelier stripling;
With half a College Education got,
Half Clown, half Prig, half Pedant and half Sot;
Having done all that ought to be undone,
Finish'd those Studies which were ne'er begun;
To foreign Climes my Lord must take his Flight.

James Miller, *On Politeness*, 1738.

53

London University Opened

At the East End of Exeter Change in the Strand, this evening at 6 o'clock will be opened the London University, where all liberal Arts and Sciences will be most usefully, critically and demonstratively taught in the mother tongue in proper courses of lectures, composed by men of the greatest learning and delivered with good address, so as to be entertaining to all and particularly improving to the ladies and such gentlemen as have not had an academical education, as more real learning will be exhibited thus in few months than in an equal number of years elsewhere. The opening lecture will be a rational view of the nature, reality, origin, extent, past and present state of all liberal Arts and Sciences with the means of improving them.

At midsummer next proper Schools will be opened in the centre of the town where very able Professors will teach all liberal Arts and sciences in the mother tongue – advertisement of 31 March 1742.

School-Boys

I have attended Westminster School and have seen Eton, which are the chief foundations of this sort. The children who are all dressed alike, in the plainest manner imaginable, and who have their hair cut like our brethren De La Charite [monks] , with a band on their necks, show how they are likely to turn out at the age of fifty. With faces which are generally speaking very handsome, and with an air of the utmost mildness, they are the most intractable and most obstinate creatures that ever came out of the hands of nature. In their deportment, in their very pastimes, their countenances show nothing of that flexible disposition and those winning graces which elsewhere are discoverable in boys of their age: they do not betray their archness by those tricks, and those little frolics, the result of which is to laugh at the expense of their school-fellows. To make up for this, they are mad for violent exercises, the want of which they already feel; to be indulged in these exercises is the greatest favour they expect from their masters. If, during their recreations, they listen to the conversation of their tutors, generally speaking this turns upon politics and either tires and disgusts them, or inspires them with an early taste for subjects of that nature.

If we follow these youths to the university, which is governed by a despotic principal, the recluse manner of living in the several colleges seems calculated to give an additional degree of stiffness and obstinacy to those haughty, harsh, and unyielding spirits rather than to soften their disposition.

As we sailed up the Thames from Windsor to Eton, at about fifty paces from the college we came to the head of a mill-bank, where were three of the grown scholars who had hid themselves amongst the reeds, to erect a little battery. We passed by them and were saluted with a general discharge which would, doubtless, have peppered us most terribly if they had been better marksmen. We were obliged to them for their good intention and arrived at the college, after having crossed a meadow which separates it from the Thames. It was then sunset, the damps began to fall and the grass was covered with a dewy moisture: yet at this very time we saw about sixty of the boys, in their shirts, dripping with sweat, and playing at cricket. A pretty youth, nearly related to the Earl of Chesterfield, upon seeing me, quitted his play and came to pay his respects. With astonishment I heard that he and his companions took this recreation every day, at the same hour and in the same place. These boys were watched by one person only, at some distance, who sat upon the banks of the Thames, with a book in his hand.

Having afterwards visited the college, which is divided into several courts, the largest adorned with a bronze statue of the founder, Henry the Sixth, we walked about the town and entered a grocer's shop, to wait the arrival of part of our company. During the short stay that we made there, about a dozen of the scholars came to buy biscuits, sugar-plums, and other sweetmeats. There was a buxom wench, belonging to the shop, whom some of those young gentlemen caressed and kissed before our faces.

I have already spoken of the quarrels which happen among those boys, especially in their walks; quarrels which, the day following or when first an opportunity offers, they decide by fisty-cuffs, with the resolution and obstinacy of boxers by profession. Scarce can the presence of the most respectable company keep the young people in awe. Could we suppose an assembly of that sort, it was surely that which met in Westminster Hall, when Lord Byron was brought to trial. At the head of the inclosure, which was set apart for peers, over whom the Lord Chancellor presided as high-steward, stood a throne, which, though it was not filled by the king, represented royal majesty in judgment. The children of the noblest families in England, dressed in little frocks which they wear at school and which confounds them with the offspring of citizens and the lower sort of people, were crowded on the steps going to the throne and seemed very attentive to the proceedings of the court. But they began afterwards to behave like themselves, as soon as the peers entered in to debate upon the several articles of the accusation; then they rolled about the steps of the throne, quarrelled, swallowed down apples, with which their pockets were crammed, and threw the remainder in each other's faces. I even saw some of them fling bits of apples into the enormous periwig of the Lord High Steward, who was the more conveniently situated for that purpose as the back of his seat was towards the throne. He turned about two or three times with a complacent air, which seemed to show that he took their freedom in good part. In a word I never saw youths behave in a less decent manner or appear less sensible of the dignity of a magistrate.

The lower choir of St. Paul's offered to my eye a sight of the same nature. It consisted of about a dozen beggarly boys, dressed in surplices which hung very slovenly, now moving to and fro, now standing still, now singing or rather squeaking, and now quite silent, as they happened to be in humour, and often making mouths at each other. It must, notwithstanding, be acknowledged that in persons of all ranks, the English education is a preservative against effeminacy, vanity and an idle life. Public education is almost the only sort known in England. Children of the first rank have private tutors who prepare them for the public schools — J. B. Le Blanc, *Letters on the English and French Nations*, 1747.

A Private School, *c.* 1750

At the Boarding-school in the Vineyard, Youth are commodiously Boarded; and taught writing in all Hands now practised, with the proper Ornaments; Arithmetic of Whole Numbers and Fractions both vulgar and Decimal; the Computation of Foreign Exchanges; and Book Keeping, either by the English or Italian Method; together with constant Instructions in the English Grammar. These several Articles taught, and Boarding included, for Twelve Guineas a Year and One guinea Entrance. There are also taught Geometry, Plain Trigonometry, and Mensuration of Superficials and Solid, also Surveying of Lands after the most accurate Manner by the Theodolite, or Circumferentor, lately purchased for that Business. But these Branches of Learning are distinct from the former, and taught for Two Guineas each.... And those who have already learnt the first four Rules of Arithmetic, may be fully compleated for Business in one year — J. Townshend, 'News of a Country Town' in *Jackson's Oxford Journal*, relating to Abingdon.

Spelling Settled by Rules

I must tell you that orthography, in the true sense of the word is so absolutely necessary for a man of letters, or a gentleman, that one false spelling may fix a ridicule upon him for the rest of his life. And I know a man of quality who never recovered the ridicule of having spelled *wholesome* without the w — Lord Chesterfield, letter to his son, 1750.

Letter-Writing

The importance of writing letters with propriety justly claims to be considered with care, since next to the power of pleasing with his presence, every man should wish to be able to give delight at a distance.

The mechanical art of writing began to be cultivated amongst us in the reign of Queen Elizabeth, and was at that time so highly valued, that it contributed much to the fame and fortune of him who wrote his pages with neatness, and embellished them with elegant draughts and illuminations; and it was partly, perhaps, to this encouragement, that we now surpass all other nations in this art — Samuel Johnson, 1750.

The Grand Tour

Persons who propose to themselves a Scheme for Travelling, generally do it with a View to obtain one or more of the following Ends, viz. *First*, to make curious Collections, as Natural Philosophers, Virtuosos, or Antiquarians. *Secondly*, to improve in Painting, Statuary, Architecture and Music, *Thirdly*, To obtain the reputation of being Men of Vertu, and of an elegant Taste. *Fourthly*, To acquire foreign Airs, and adorn their dear Persons with fine Cloaths and new Fashions, and their

Conversation with new Phrases. Or *Fifthly*, To rub off local Prejudices (which is indeed the most commendable Motive, though not the most prevailing) and to acquire that impartial view of Men and Things, which no one single Country can afford.... As to that Species of Beings found only here in England (a Country of universal Freedom and Opulence) who go abroad with no other view but because they are tired of staying at Home, and can afford to make themselves as ridiculous every where as they please: It would be a Loss of Time to take any other Notice of them, than just to observe, that they are sure of returning Home as Wise as they went out, but much more Impertinent, less Wealthy, and less Innocent – Dean Tucker, *Instructions for Travellers*, 1757.

Boarding-School for Young Ladies

... boarded and instructed in the Rudiments of the English Tongue, and taught Dresden and all manner of Needle Work in the neatest Manner for £11 a year, and Two Guineas Entrance. The utmost Care and Attention are had to their Conduct and Behaviour in general, as well as to their Improvement in the above mentioned Particulars. Writing, French, Music and Dancing are also taught at the same school at an additional, but easy Expense – advertisement, Abingdon, August 1758.

Education of Girls

I beg your assistance to convey some hints on a subject I do not remember to have seen yet treated of, which, though it cannot be considered in the light of the above charities, is nevertheless of some consequence. I mean the improper education given to a great number of the daughters of low tradesmen and mechanics. Every village in the neighbourhood of this great city has one or two little boarding schools, with an inscription over the door, 'Young ladies boarded and educated.' The expense is small, and hither the blacksmith, the ale-house keeper, the shoemaker etc., sends his daughter, who, from the moment she enters these walls, becomes a young lady. The parent's intention is an honest one: his time is too much taken up, as well as his wife's, by the necessary duties of their profession, to have any to bestow on the education of their children; they are therefore obliged to send them from home. As this is the case, there ought certainly to be proper schools for their reception: but surely, the plan of these schools ought to differ as much from that of the great schools, intended for the daughters of the nobility and gentry, as the station in life of the scholars at the one, differs from those of the other. This is however so far from being the case, that the article of expense excepted, the plan is the same, and the daughter of the lowest shopkeeper at one of these schools, is as much Miss, and a young lady, as the daughter of the first Viscount in England, at one of the other. The mistress of the school is called governess, for the word Mistress has a vulgar sound with it: and Miss, whose mamma sells oysters, tells Miss, whose papa deals in smallcoal, that her governess shall know it, if she spits in her face, or does anything else unbecoming a young lady. Was a foreigner acquainted with our language, to overhear a conversation of this kind, and some such conversation is to be heard every day in some alley or other in this town, how would he be astonished at the opulence of a country, where the meanest tradesmen kept governesses for their daughters. French and dancing is also to be taught at these schools, neither of which can be of any use to young ladies of this sort. The parents may imagine the first may procure them a place, but in this they may be greatly mistaken as, I believe, there is hardly a single instance of a girl's having learnt that language to any degree of perfection at one of these schools. As to the last, I could give reasons against that accomplishment making a part of their education far too numerous to be inserted. I shall only mention that it cannot possibly be of use to them, and that it would be of much more consequence they should be well instructed how to wash the floor than how to dance upon it. I am very certain there are several fathers of this rank who have had cause to wish their daughters had lost the use of their limbs, rather than been taught this pernicious use of them by the dancing master, the consequence of which has often been that of inducing them to quit their parents' sober dwelling at a midnight hour for the licentious liberties of a ball of 'prentices, where the young lady, no governess present, may be exposed to great dangers. The needlework taught at these schools is of a kind much more likely to strengthen the natural propensity in all young minds to show and dress, than to answer any housewifely purpose. One of these young ladies, with the assistance of an ounce of coarse thread and a yard of cat gut, dresses herself up in what has the appearance of point or

Brussels lace.

How disappointed will the honest shopkeeper be, if, at an age when he thinks proper to take his daughter from school, he should expect any assistance from her! Can he suppose a young lady will weigh his soap for him? Or perform any other office the gentility of her education has exalted her so far above? Though ignorant of everything else, she will be so perfect in the lessons of pride and vanity, that she will despise him and his nasty shop, and quit both, to go off with the first man who promises her a silk gown and a blonde cap. . . . I would propose that schools for the education of such girls should be kept by discreet women; those who have been housekeepers in large families would be the properest persons for this purpose: that the young people should be taught submission and humility to their superiors, decency and modesty in their own dress and behaviour. That they should be very well instructed in all kinds of plain-work, reading, writing, accompts, pastry, pickling, preserving, and other branches of cookery; be taught to weave, and wash lace and other linen. Thus instructed, they may be of great comfort and assistance to their parents and husbands; they may have a right to expect the kindest treatment from their mistresses; they are sure to be respected as useful members of society; whereas young ladies are the most useless of all God's creatures — *Annual Register*, 1759.

6 The Arts

MUSIC

The City Waits, Topping Tooters

We heard a noise so dreadful and surprising, that we thought the Devil was riding or hunting through the City, with a pack of deep-mouth'd hell-hounds, to catch a brace of tallymen for breakfast. At last bolted out from the corner of a street, with an Ignis Fatuus dancing before them, a parcel of strange hobgoblins cover'd with long frize rugs and blankets, hoop'd round with leather girdles from their cruppers to their shoulders and their noodles button'd up into caps of martial figure, like a knight-errant at tilt and tournament, with his wooden head lock'd in an iron helmet; one arm'd, as I thought, with a lusty faggot-bat, and the rest with strange wooden weapons in their hands in the shape of clyster-pipes, but as long, almost, as speaking trumpets. Of a sudden they clapp'd them to their mouths, and made such a frightful yelling that I thought the world had been dissolving, and the terrible sound of the last trumpet to be within an inch of my ears. Under these amazing apprehensions, I ask'd my friend what was the meaning of this infernal outcry? Prithee, says he, what's the matter with thee? Thou look'st as if thou were Gally'd; why these are the City Waits, who play every winter's night through the streets, to rouse each lazy drone to family duty.... These are the Topping Tooters of the Town; and have gowns, silver chains, and salaries for playing Lilla Burlera to my Lord Mayor's Horse through the City — Ned Ward, *The London Spy*, 1698–1709.

Italian Singers Presenting Handel's
'Lotario and Partenope'

Bernacchi has a vast compass, his voice mellow and clear, but not so
sweet as Senesino, his manner better; his person not so good, for he
is as big as a Spanish friar. Fabri has a tenor voice, sweet, clear, and
firm, but not strong enough, I doubt, for the stage: he sings like a
gentleman, without making faces, and his manner is particularly agreeable; he is the greatest master of music that ever sung upon the stage.
The third is the bass, a very good distinct voice, without any harshness.
La Strada is the first woman; her voice is without exception fine, her
manner near perfection, but her person is *very bad*, and she makes
frightful mouths. La Merighi is the next to her; her voice is not so
extraordinarily good or bad, she is tall and has a very graceful person,
with a tolerable face: she seems to be a woman about forty, she sings
easily and agreeably. The last is Bertoli, she has neither voice, ear,
nor manner to recommend her; but she is a perfect beauty, quite a
Cleopatra, that sort of complexion with regular features, fine teeth,
and when she sings has a smile about her mouth which is extreme
pretty, and I believe has practised to sing before a glass, for she has
never any distortion of her face – letter from Mrs Pendarves to Anne
Granville, 1728.

George Handel's Maggots

Mr. Handel's head is more full of maggots than ever. I found yesterday
in his room a very queer instrument which he calls carillon (Anglice,
a bell) and says some call it a Tubalcain, I suppose because it is both in
the make and tone like a set of Hammers striking upon anvils. 'Tis
played upon with keys like a Harpsichord and with this Cyclopean
instrument he designs to make poor Saul mad. His second maggot is
an organ of £500 price which (because he is overstocked with money)
he has bespoke of one Moss of Barnet. This organ, he says, is so constructed that as he sits at it he has a better command of his performers
than he used to have, and he is highly delighted to think with what
exactness his Oratorio will be performed by the help of this organ;
so that for the future instead of beating time at his oratorios, he is to
sit at the organ all the time with his back to his Audience.

His third maggot is a Hallelujah which he has trump'd up at the end of his oratorio since I went into the Country, because he thought the conclusion of the oratorio not Grand enough; tho' if that were the case 'twas his own fault, for the words would have bore as Grand Music as he could have set 'em to: but this Hallelujah, Grand as it is, comes in very nonsensically, having no manner of relation to what goes before. And this is the more extraordinary, because he refused to set a Hallelujah at the end of the first Chorus of the Oratorio, where I had placed one and where it was to be introduced with the utmost propriety, upon a pretence that it would make the entertainment too long. I could tell you more of his maggots: but it grows late and I must defer the rest till I write next, by which time, I doubt not, more new ones will breed in his brain — Charles Jennens, letter to the Earl of Guernsey, 19 September 1738.

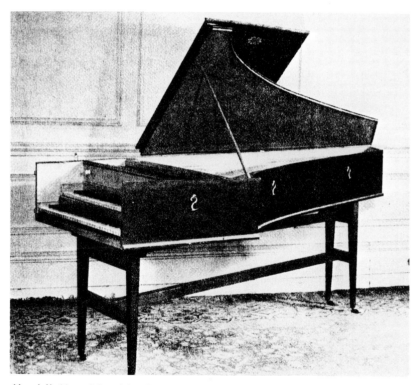

Handel's Harpsichord, by Joannes Ruckers. Although made in the seventeenth century it has always been associated with Handel. He published eight suites for harpsichord in 1720.

First Performance of 'The Messiah', 13 April 1741

On Tuesday last Mr. Handel's Sacred Grand Oratorio, *The Messiah* was performed in the New Music Hall in Fishamble Street; the best judges allowed it to be the most finished piece of Music. Words are wanting to express the exquisite delight it afforded to the admiring crowded audience. The sublime, the grand, and the tender, adapted to the most elevated, majestic and moving words, conspired to transport and charm the ravished heart and ear. It is but justice to Mr. Handel that the world should know he generously gave the money arising from this grand performance, to be equally shared by the Society for relieving Prisoners, the Charitable Infirmary, and Mercer's Hospital, for which they will ever gratefully remember his name; and that the Gentlemen of the Two Choirs [Christ Church and St. Patrick's] Mr. Duburg, Mrs. Avolio, and Mrs. Cibber, who all performed their parts to admiration acted also on the same disinterested principle, satisfied with the deserved applause of the public, and the conscious pleasure of promoting such useful and extensive charity. There were above 700 people in the room, and the sum collected amounted to about £400, out of which £127 goes to each of the three great and pious charities — *Faulkner's Journal*.

PAINTING

A Private Exhibition

Mr. Highmore proposes to publish by subscription twelve prints by the best French engravers after his own paintings, representing the most remarkable adventures of Pamela; in which he has endeavoured to comprehend her whole story as well as to preserve a connection between the several pictures, which follow each other as parts successive and dependent, so as to complete the subject. This is more distinctly illustrated in the account attached to the proposals, wherein all the twelve pictures are described and their respective connections shown. All the pictures being now completed and to be seen at Mr. Highmore's house, the Two Lyons, Lincoln's Inn Fields — *London Evening Post*, 1744.

After Duty, by Richard Newton.
'The death of Richard Newton, at the age of twenty-one, robbed
England of a caricaturist who, in his maturity, might have become the
greatest of them all. Many of his most brilliant satires were produced by
him between the age of eleven and sixteen.' From a contemporary print.

Painting

The present State of this Art in Britain does not afford sufficient education to the painter. We have but one Academy meanly supported by the
private subscriptions of the students, in all this great metropolis. There
they have but two figures, a man and a woman, and consequently there
can be but little experience gathered. The subscribers to this lone Academy pay two guineas a season which goes to the expense of the room
and lights. The subscribers in their turn set the figure, that is place the
man and woman in such atittude in the middle of the room as suits
their fancy. He who sets the figures chooses what seat he likes and all
the rest take their places according as they stand in the list and then
proceed to drawing, every man according to his prospect of the figure —
The London Tradesman, 1747.

Art is a Form of Satire

The leading points in these, as well as in *Beer Street* and *Gin Lane* were made as obvious as possible, in the hope that their tendency might be seen by men of the lowest rank and the fact is that the passions may be more forcibly expresst by a strong bold stroke, than by the most delicate engraving. To expressing them as I felt them, I have paid the utmost attention, and as they were addresst to hard hearts, have rather preferred leaving them hard — William Hogarth, Note to *The Four Stages of Cruelty*, 1751.

Michael Rysbrack's model for his famous *Hercules* at Stourhead, 1756. Horace Walpole praises the statue 'compiled from the various limbs of seven or eight of the strongest and best made men in London, chiefly the bruisers and boxers of the then flourishing amphitheatre for boxing, the sculptor selecting the parts which were most truly formed in each'.

THEATRE

Dangers of Play-Going in Eighteenth-Century London

In our playhouses at London, besides an Upper-Gallery for footmen, coachmen, mendicants, etc, we have three other different and distinct classes; the first is called the Boxes, where there is one peculiar to the King and Royal Family, and the rest for the persons of quality, and for the ladies and gentlemen of the highest rank, unless some fools that have more wit than money, or perhaps more impudence than both, crowd in among them. The second is call'd the Pit, where sit the judges, wits and censurers, or rather the censurers without either wit or judgment . . . In common with these sit the squires, sharpers, beaus, bullies, and whores, and here and there an extravagant male and female citizen. The third is distinguished by the title of the Middle Gallery, where the citizens wives and daughters, together with the abigails, serving-men, journey-men and apprentices commonly take their places; and now and then some desponding mistresses and superannuated poets.

Well, when you come there, the eyes of every body are presently upon you, especially the whores and sharpers, who immediately, give out the word, to try if any body knows you; and if they find you are a stranger, then a lady in a mask, alias whore which (as they express it), is a good tongue-pad, is forthwith detach'd to go and sound you, and in the meantime a cabal of bullies and sharpers are consulting which way you must be manag'd, and passing their judgments upon you. The lady comes up to you with a kind of formal impudence, and fixes herself as near you as she can, and then begins some loose and impertinent prate, to draw you into discourse with her. If she finds you a man fit for their turn, and a true squire, with some sort of subtle and insinuating civility, she leaves you a little to go and make her report to her friends and allies, that are earnestly waiting to know the success of her negotiation, in another part of the pit . . . If they find their whore can do no good with you, then they try another expedient; an ingenious gentleman that's born westward of England makes up to you, and he, forsooth, must know what countryman you are, or what's a clock by your watch? Or what part of the town you lodge in, or where you sup? These sort of sparks are commonly well stock'd with confidence and impertinence, and so don't stand much upon forms and ceremonies with you; but, by his soul, if you'll go along with him to the tavern and drink an honest gentleman's health he can carry you to a glass of the best wine in London. If he can wheedle you thither, first to make you drunk, then to draw you into gaming, and then by the help of his false dice, and other tricks and slights of hand, the only arts that he is master of, he soon gets your ready money, takes your notes for more, by which means he links you so fast to him that without the greatest caution, you are insensibly ruin'd before you can disentangle yourself — from *The Tricks of the Town Laid Open*, a contemporary pamphlet.

Strolling Players Dressing in a Barn, from an engraving by William Hogarth, 1738. Here is a contrast between the poor players in this setting and their display on the stage. Play-bills announce 'The Devil to pay in Heaven' to be acted on the George Inn.

Transformation Scenes at Covent Garden

Mr Rich, the director of this theatre, spends a great deal of money on plays of this sort; two well-known ones are the *Rape of Europa* and *Orpheus in the Lower Regions*. In the former play a part of the theatre represents hell, in which are seated gods and goddesses; it rises gradually into the clouds; at the same instant out of the earth rises another stage. The scene represents a farmhouse, in front of which is a dunghill with an egg, the size of an ostrich's, on it. This egg, owing to the heat of the sun, grows gradually larger and larger; when it is of a very large size it cracks open, and a little Harlequin comes out of it. He is of the size of a child of three to four years old, and little by little attains a natural height. It is said Mr Rich spent more than £4,000 sterling on *Orpheus*. The serpent that kills Eurydice is of enormous size, and is covered all over with gold and green scales and with red spots; his eyes shine like fire, and he wriggles about the theatre with head upraised, making an awful but very natural hissing noise. The first night this pantomime was given, the King was there, and I had the good fortune to be present. One of the two Grenadiers of the guard, who are posted at either side of the stage with their backs turned to the actors, noticed the serpent only when he was at his feet, and this reptile was so natural that the man dropped his musket, and drawing his sword made as though he would cut the monster in two. I do not know whether the soldier was really alarmed or whether he was acting, but if so it was admirably done, and the spectators laughed again and again. This piece is full of wonderful springs and clockwork machinery. When Orpheus learns that his beloved is dead, he retires into the depth of the stage and plays on his lyre; presently out of the rocks appear little bushes; they gradually grow up into trees, so that the stage resembles a forest. On these trees flowers blossom, then fall off, and are replaced by different fruits, which you see grow and ripen. Wild beasts, lions, bears, tigers creep out of the forest attracted by Orpheus and his lyre. It is altogether the most surprising and charming spectacle you can imagine – César de Saussure, *A Foreign View of England in the Reigns of George I and George II*, 1725-9.

The Beggar's Opera

Dr. Swift had been observing once to Mr. Gay, what an odd pretty sort of thing a Newgate Pastoral might make. Gay was inclined to try at such a thing for some time, but afterwards thought it would be better to write a comedy on the same plan. This was what gave rise to the *Beggar's Opera*. He began on it, and when he first mentioned it to Swift, the Doctor did not much like the project. As he carried it on, he showed what he wrote to both of us, and we now and then gave a correction, or a word or two of advice; but it was wholly of his own writing. When it was done, neither of us thought it would succeed. We showed it to Congreve, who, after reading it over, said, 'It would either take greatly, or be damned confoundedly.'

[Gay offered the *Beggar's Opera* to Colley Cibber for Drury Lane Theatre. Cibber, however, rejected it. Gay then took it to Rich, at the

A scene from John Gay's *The Beggar's Opera*. Some of the audience are on the stage. From an engraving by William Hogarth, 1730.

Lincoln's Inn Fields Theatre, where it was produced on 27 January 1728.]

We were all at the first night of it in great uncertainty of the event, till we were being much encouraged by overhearing the Duke of Argyle, who sat in the next box to us, say, 'It will do — it must do! I see it in the eyes of them.' This was a good while before the first act was over, and so gave us ease soon; for the Duke, besides his own good taste, has a more particular knack than any one now living in discovering the taste of the public. He was quite right in this, as usual; the good nature of the audience appeared stronger and stronger every act, and ended with a clamour of applause.

So early as the 20th of March, when the piece had only been acted thirty-two times, the receipts had been £5351, 15s. Hence it is said that the play had made Rich *gay*, and Gay *rich* — Joseph Spence, *Anecdotes*, 1728.

7 Sports and Pastimes

At the Bear-Garden in Hockley in the Hole, near Clarken-Well-Green

These are to give Notice to all Gentlemen and Gamesters, that this present Monday, there will be a Match fought out by four Dogs, two of Westminster against two of Eastcheap, at the Bull, for a Guinea.

And a Mad Bull let loose to be baited, with fireworks all over him, and Dogs after him.

With other Variety of Bull Baiting and Bear Baiting. Being a general day of Sport by all the Old Gamesters.

Beginning at Three a Clock The Gentlemen are desired to come betimes because the Sport will be long — 1715.

Cudgelling in the West Country

Wednesday, June 15, 1715. Dined at brother's. Met there with Cousin Billio and his wife. She is very big, it makes her look a little dull and heavy. Sat with her alone half an hour. We found it very difficult to find discourse for so long a time. We seemed both uneasy.

Went to our club. Mr. Samson told us of a very odd sort of custom in the West of England. Cudgelling is a mighty diversion among them and it's handed down from father to son. The father teaches his sons to cudgel by playing with them himself and never allows them to spare him, but when they have once broke his head he then thinks them fit to shift for themselves and go into the world.

There was a father cudgelling with his son and the young man was afraid to strike his father who continually pressed him to it. 'Sirrah,' says he, 'why don't you strike me?' But the boy refused until his father at length gave him a smart blow that raised his spirits and the young rogue had courage enough to break his father's head. 'That is well done,' says the father. 'Now you are fit to go into the world.'

It seems they beat one another most furiously, and the father will set his children to cudgel and stand by and encourage them to thrash one another — Dudley Ryder, *Diary*, 1715-16.

Sports and Diversions

Besides the Sports and Diversions common to most other *European* Nations, as Tennis, Billiards, Chess, Tick-Tack, Dancing, Plays etc., the *English* have some which are particular to them, or at least which they love and use more than any other People. Cock-fighting is a Royal Pleasure in *England*. Their Combates between Bulls and Dogs, Bears and Dogs, and sometimes Bulls and Bears, are not Battals to Death, as those of Cocks: Anything that looks like Fighting is delicious to an *Englishman*. If two little Boys quarrel in the Street, then Passengers stop, make a Ring round them in a Moment, and set them against one another, that they may come to Fisticuffs. When 'tis come to a Fight, each pulls off his Neckcloth and his Waistcoat (some will strip themselves quite naked to their Wastes), and give them to hold to some of the Standers-by; then they begin to brandish their Fists in the Air; the Blows are aim'd all at the Face, they kick one another's Shins, they tug one another by the Hair etc. He that has got the other down, may give him one Blow or two before he rises, but no more; and let the Boy get up ever so often, the other is oblig'd to box him again as often as he requires it. During the Fight, the Ring of By-standers encourage the Combatants with great Delight of Heart, and never part them while they fight according to the Rules: and these By-standers are not only other Boys, Porters and Rabble, but all Sorts of Men of Fashion; some thrusting by the Mob that they may see plain, others sitting upon Stalls; and all would hire places if Scaffolds could be built in a Moment. ... These Combats are less frequent among grown Men than Children, but they are not rare ... Wrestling too is one of the Diversions of the English, especially in the Northern Counties. . . . In Winter *Footballs* is a useful and charming Exercise: it is a Leather Ball about as big as one's Head, fill'd with Wind: This is kick'd about from one to t'other in the Streets, by him that can get at it, and that is all the Art of it. Setting up a Cock in some open Place, and knocking it down with a Stick, at forty or fifty Paces Distance, is another Sport that affords no little Pleasure; but this Diversion is confin'd to a certain Season — M. Misson, *Memoirs and Observations*, 1719.

Bull-Baiting

Here follows the manner of those bull-baitings which are so much talked of:— They tie a rope to the root of the horns of the ox or bull, and fasten the other end of the cord to an iron ring fixed to a stake driven into the ground; so that this cord being about 15 feet long, the bull is confined to a sphere of about 30 foot diameter. Several butchers, or other gentlemen, that are desirous to exercise their dogs, stand round about, each holding his own by the ears, and when the sport begins, they let loose one of the dogs. The dog runs at the bull; the bull immovable looks down upon the dog with an eye of scorn and only turns a horn to him to hinder him from coming near. The dog is not daunted at this; he runs round him and tries to get beneath his belly in order to seize him by the muzzle or the dewlap. The bull then puts himself into a posture of defence. He beats the ground with his feet, which he joins together as close as possible, and his chief aim is not to gore the dog with the point of his horn (when the bull's horns are too sharp they put them into a kind of wooden sheath) but to slide one of them under the dog's belly (who creeps close to the ground to hinder it), and to throw him so high in the air that he may break his neck in the fall. This often happens. When the dog thinks he is sure of fixing his teeth, a turn of the horn, which seems to be done with all the negligence in the world, gives him a sprawl thirty feet high, and puts him in danger of a damnable squelch when he comes down. This danger would be unavoidable if the dog's friends were not ready beneath him, some with their backs to give him a soft reception, and others with long poles, which they offer him slantways, so that sliding down them, it may break the force of his fall. Notwithstanding all this care, a toss generally makes him sing to a very scurvy tune and draw his phiz into a pitiful grimace. But unless he is totally stunned with the fall, he is sure to crawl again towards the bull, with his old antipathy, come on't what will. Sometimes a second frisk into the air disables him for ever from playing his old tricks. But sometimes too, he fastens upon his enemy and when once he has seized him with his eye-teeth, he sticks to him like a leech and would sooner die than leave his hold. Then the bull bellows and bounds and kicks about to shake off the dog. By his leaping the dog seems to be no manner of weight to him, though in all appearance he puts him to great pain. In the end, either the dog tears out the piece he has laid hold on, and falls, or else remains fixed to him with an obstinacy that would never end if they did not pull him off.

To call him away would be in vain; to give him a hundred blows would be as much so; you might cut him to pieces joint by joint before he would let him loose. What is to be done then? While some hold the bull, others thrust staves into the dog's mouth and open it by main force. This is the only way to part them — M. Misson, *Memoirs and Observations*, 1719.

Cock-Fighting

They are large but short-legged birds, their feathers are scarce, they have no crests to speak of, and are very ugly to look at. Some of these fighting-cocks are celebrated, and have pedigrees like gentlemen of good family, some of them being worth five or six guineas. I am told that when transported to France they degenerate — their strength and courage disappear, and they become like ordinary cocks.

The stage on which they fight is round and small. One of the cocks is released, and struts about proudly for a few seconds. He is then caught up and his enemy appears. When the bets are made, one of the cocks is placed on either end of the stage; they are armed with silver spurs, and immediately rush at each other and fight furiously. It is surprising to see the ardour, the strength, and courage of these little birds, for they rarely give up till one of them is dead. The spectators are ordinarily composed of common people, and the noise is terrible, and it is impossible to hear yourself speak unless you shout. At Whitehall Cockpit, on the contrary, where the spectators are mostly people of a certain rank, the noise is much less; but would you believe that at this place several hundred pounds are sometimes lost and won? Cocks will sometimes fight a whole hour before one or other is victorious; at other times one may get killed at once. You sometimes see a cock ready to fall and apparently die, seeming to have no more strength, and suddenly it will regain all its vigour, fight with renewed courage, and kill his enemy. Sometimes a cock will be seen vanquishing his opponent, and, thinking he is dead (if cocks can think), jump on the body of the bird and crow lustily with triumph, when the fallen bird will unexpectedly revive and slay the victor. Of course, such cases are very rare, but their possibility makes the fight very exciting — César de Saussure, *A Foreign View of England in the Reigns of George I and George II*, 1725-9.

Male and Female Gladiators

The gladiators' stage is round, the spectators sit in galleries, and the spectacle generally commences by a fight with wicker staves by a few rogues. They do not spare each other, but are very skilful in giving great whacks on the head. When blood oozes from one of the combatants, a few coins are thrown to the victor. These games serve to pass the time till all the spectators have arrived. The day I went to see the gladiators fight I witnessed an extraordinary combat, two women being the champions. . . . Their weapons were a sort of two-handed sword, three or three and a half feet in length; the guard was covered, and the blade was about three inches wide and not sharp – only about half a foot of it was, but then that part cut like a razor. The spectators made numerous bets, and, some peers who were there, some very large wagers. . . . Two male champions next appeared. They wore short white jackets and breeches and hose of the same colour; their heads were bare and freshly shaven; one of them wore green ribbons, the other yellow. They were hideous to look at, their faces being all seamed and scarred. They commenced by paying each other grotesque and amusing compliments, and then fell on each other with the same sort of weapons the women had used; but they showed more strength, vigour, and ability, if not more courage. One blow rapidly followed another; it was really surprising neither man should be killed, but this never seems to happen. They fought five or six times running, and only stopped for the sewing up of a wound or when too exhausted to continue. After every round the victor was thrown money by his backers; but he had to exercise great skill in catching the coins, for he had a right only to those he caught in his hands; those that fell on the ground became the property of some of the numerous rascals that were standing about, who hastened to pick them up and appropriate them. The two combatants received several wounds, one of them having his ear nearly severed from his head, and a few moments later his opponent got a cut across the face, commencing at the left eye and ending on the right cheek. This last wound ended the fight and entertainment, and I went away regretting my half-crown and determined never to assist at one of these combats again – César de Saussure, *A Foreign View of England in the Reigns of George I and George II*, 1725-9.

Perils of Football

Another amusement which is very inconvenient to passers-by is football. For this game a leather ball filled with air is used, and is kicked about with the feet. In cold weather you sometimes see a score of rascals in the streets kicking at a ball, and they will break panes of glass and smash the windows of coaches, and also knock you down without the slightest compunction; on the contrary they will roar with laughter — César de Saussure, letter to Swiss friend, 1727.

Gaming and Duelling in Bath

Bath, October 31. This morning, between 10 and 11, a duel was fought with pistols in Harrison's Walks, between Mr Bazil Prise of this city, merchant, second son of Will Prise, Esq; formerly Knight of the shire for the county of Hereford, and one Mr Charles Jones, late a fellow of New College in Oxford, who about five years since quitted his fellowship, and came down here with £200 and won upwards of £4000, but his good fortune not continuing, was reduced to the stage. The night before, Mr Prise and he were at a billiard table, and agreed to play a game for half a crown, which Mr Prise won, and demanded his money. But Jones said he would owe him half a crown. Whereupon Mr Prise growing angry, kicked him down stairs. Jones went out of the house, and wrote him a challenge. Mr Prise discharged his pistol first, but missed him. When Jones, as it is said, went up to him, and shot him under the right breast, so that he never spoke afterwards, but expired in about ten minutes. Jones made his escape immediately. The Coroner's inquest brought in their verdict Wilful Murder, the challenge being found in Mr Prise's pocket — *The Grub-street Journal*, 11 November 1731.

The Craze for Gambling

Feb. 3, 1743/4. Lord Montford betts Mr Wardour twenty guineas on each, that Mr Shepherd outlives Sir Hans Sloan, the Duchess Dowager of Marlborough, and Duke of Somerset.—Voide.

Mr Jno Jeffreys betts Mr Stephen Jansen fifty guineas, that thirteen members of Parliament don't die from the first of Jany 1744/5 to the first of Jany 1745/6 exclusive of what may be killed in battle.

Ld Leicester betts Lord Montfort one hundred guineas that six or more Peers of the British Parliament, including Catholics, Minors, Bishops, and sixteen Scotch Lords, shall die between the 2 of Dec 1744, and the first of Dec 1745 inclusive.

16 *July*, 1746. Mr Heath wagers Mr Fanshawe five guineas that the eldest son of the Pretender is dead, on, or before this day. To be returned if the Pretender was dead.—pd. Nov 28.

Octr 20, 1746. Mr Heath gave Col Perry twenty pounds, for which Col Perry is to pay Mr Heath one hundred pounds if ever he loses more than one hundred pounds in any four and twenty hours.

Nov. 14, 1746. Mr Fox betts Mr John Jeffreys five guineas on November Two against number one in the present lottery.

Lord Montford wagers Sir Wm. Stanhope twenty guineas that Lady Mary Coke has a child before Ly Kildare, and twenty guineas more that Ly Mary Coke has a child before Ly Fawkner.

January the 14, 1747/8. Mr Fanshawe wagers Lord Dalkeith one guinea, that his peruke is better than his Lordship's, to be judged by the majority of members the next time they both shall meet — entries for the years from 1743 to 1747/8 from the betting book of White's Club, London.

A Gaming-House Keeper

I, Dame Mary, Baroness of Mordington, do hold a house in the Great Piazza, Covent Garden, for and as an Assembly, where all persons of credit are at liberty to frequent and play at such diversions as are used at other Assemblys. And I have hired Joseph Dewberry, William Horsely, Ham Cropper, and George Sanders, as my servants, or managers (under me), thereof. . . . And all the above mentioned persons I claim as my servants, and demand all those privileges that belong to me, as a Peeress of Great Britain, appertaining to my said Assembly — M. Mordington. Dated 8 Jan. 1745

Jubilee-Masquerade

The Peace of 1749, when the War of the Austrian Succession ended, was celebrated in London by a 'Jubilee-Masquerade in the Venetian manner' at Ranelagh, which had been opened about seven years. The fete, which had nothing Venetian about it, is described by Horace Walpole on May 3rd:

... the prettiest spectacle I ever saw; nothing in a fairy-tale surpassed it. It began at three o'clock, and about five, people of fashion began to go. When you entered you found the whole garden filled with marquees and spread with tents, which remained all night, very commodely. In one quarter was a Maypole with garlands, and people dancing round it to a tabor and pipe and rustic music, all masked, as were all the various bands of music that were disposed in different parts of the gardens; some like huntsmen with French horns, some like peasants, and a troop of harlequins and scaramouches in the little open temple on the Mount. In the canal was a sort of gondola, adorned with flags and streamers, and filled with music, rowing about. All around the outside of the amphitheatre were shops, filled with Dresden china, japan, etc., and all the shop-keepers in masks. The amphitheatre was illuminated, and in the middle was a circular bower, composed of all kinds of firs, in tubs, from twenty to thirty feet high; under them orange trees, with small lamps in each orange, and below them all sorts of the finest auriculas in pots; and festoons of natural flowers hanging from tree to tree. Between the arches, too, were firs, and smaller ones in the balconies above. There were booths for tea and wine, gaming tables and dancing, and about two thousand persons. In short, it pleased me more than anything I ever saw. It is to be once more, and probably as to dresses, as there has since been a subscription masquerade, people will go in their rich habits.

The next day were the fireworks, which by no means answered the expense, the length of preparation, and the expectation that has been raised: indeed, for a week before, the town was like a country fair, the streets filled from morning to night, scaffolds building wherever you could or could not see, and coaches arriving from every corner of the kingdom. This merry and lively scene, with the sight of the immense crowd in the Park, and on every house, the guards, and the machine itself, which was very beautiful, was all that was worth seeing. The rockets, and whatever was thrown up into the air, succeeded mighty well; but the Catherine-wheels, and all that was to compose the principal part, were pitiful and ill-conducted, with no changes of coloured fires and shapes: the illumination was mean, and lighted so slowly, that scarce anybody had patience to wait the finishing; and then what contributed to the awkwardness of the whole was the right pavilion catching fire, and being burnt down in the middle of the show. The King, the Duke, and Princess Emily saw it from the Library, with them humorously diverted with a new entertainment, called 'Harlequin Turned Philosopher, or the Country Squire Outwitted.'

8 Health

Advertisement

This is from The Charitable Surgeon, *a book by T.C. Surgeon, published by Edmund Curll in 1708. The medicines could be procured at the shop of Edmund Curll.*

Note, all the medicines prescribed in this book, are prepared by the author's own hands, and are left by him at Mr. Edmund Curll's a bookseller, at the Peacock without Temple Bar, where this book is sold. At which place, and nowhere else, they are always ready to be had, and will be delivered to any messenger that shall but ask for them by their names or numbers, or both, and pay the prices, as mentioned for each, in the following catalogue, viz.

	s.	d.
Numb. 1. The Purging Electuary,	5.	0.
Numb. 2. The Diuretic Powder,	5.	0.
Numb. 3. The Strengthening Electuary,	5.	0.
Numb. 4. The Anodyne Injection,	3.	6.
Numb. 5. The Anodyne Fotus,	3.	6.
Numb. 6. The Anodyne Powder,	4.	0.
Numb. 7. The Emetic Potion,	3.	6.
Numb. 8. The Healing Lotion,	3.	0.
Numb. 9. The Suppurating Plaster and Digestive Balsam each	2.	6.
Numb. 10. The Emetic Bolus,	3.	6.
Numb. 11. The Specific Electuary,	7.	6.
Numb. 12. The Cooling Gargle,	3.	6.
Numb. 13. The Detersive Injection,	3.	6.
Numb. 14. The Grand Preservative,	7.	6.
Numb. 15. The Sudorific Potion,	5.	0.
The Yard Syringe,	1.	0.
The Womb Syringe,	2.	0.
The Nose Syringe,	1.	0.
The Throat Syringe,	1.	0.

Note, for the greater conveniency of the patient, all these syringes may be had ready fitted for use (because not so at the pewterers), and sealed up with the same seal as the medicines are, where this book is sold.

N.B. Ask for the Yard Syringe by the name of the least syringe, and the womb syringe the great syringe.

Some general Directions in taking and applying the Medicines.

If by often taking the electuary the taste should seem in any way disgustful to the palate or stomach, or if you cannot well take it from the point of a knife as usual, then pour a little syrup of marshmallows, poppies, or what else you like best, into a spoon; then put your electuary in the syrup from off the point of a knife, pouring a little more of the same syrup over it, and sup it off. By this means you will not taste the electuary; and thus you may take the bolus.

When you use either of the syringes, you must put the end of the syringe in the liquor you would inject, and therein draw the squirt to and fro till you find it makes a good stream.

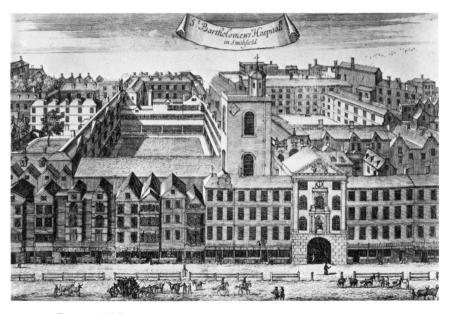

From a 1720 engraving of St Bartholomew's Hospital in Smithfield, London. Rahere began to build St Bartholomew's Hospital in 1123. By the eighteenth century it was famous for its teaching and practice.

Bodies Used on which to Demonstrate Anatomy

Our Master acquainting the Court that Mr. William Cheselden, a Member of the company did frequently procure the dead bodies of Malefactors from the place of execution and dissect the same at his own house, as well during the Company's Public Lecture as at other times, without the leave of the Governors and contrary to the Company's Bye-Laws in that belief, By which means it becomes more difficult for the Beadles to bring away the Companies Bodies and likewise draws away the Members of this Company and others from the Public Dissections and lectures at the Hall. The said Mr. Cheselden was thereupon called in. But having submitted himself to the pleasure of the Court with a promise never to dissect at the same time as the Company had its lectures at the Hall nor without the leave of the Governors for the time being, the said Mr. Cheselden was excused for what had passed with a reproof for the same pronounced by the Master at the desire of the Court — Minute in the records of the Court of Assistants, 25 March 1714.

Inoculation Against Small-Pox, 1716

A propos of distempers, I am going to tell you a thing that I am sure will make you wish yourself here. The small-pox, so fatal, and so general amongst us, is here [in Turkey] entirely harmless by the invention of ingrafting which is the term they give it. There is a set of old women who make it their business to perform the operation every autumn, in the month of September, when the great heat is abated. People send to one another to know if any of their family has a mind to have the small-pox: they make parties for this purpose, and when they are met (commonly fifteen or sixteen together), the old woman comes with a nutshell full of the matter of the best sort of small-pox and asks what veins you please to have opened. She immediately rips open that you offer to her with a large needle (which gives you no more pain than a common scratch), and puts into the vein as much venom as can lie upon the head of her needle, and after binds up the little wound with a hollow bit of shell; and in this manner opens four or five veins. The Grecians have commonly the superstition of opening one in the middle of the forehead, in each arm, and on the breast, to make the sign of the cross; but this has a very ill effect, all these wounds leaving little scars, and is not done by those that are not superstitious, who choose to have them in the legs, or that part of the arm that is concealed. The children or young patients play together all the rest of the day, and are in perfect health to the eighth. Then the fever begins to seize them, and they keep their beds two days, very seldom three. They have very rarely above twenty or thirty in their faces, which never mark; and in eight days' time they are as well as before their illness. Where they are wounded, there remain running sores during the distemper, which I don't doubt is a great relief to it. Every year thousands undergo this operation; and the French ambassador says pleasantly, that they take the small-pox here by way of diversion, as they take the waters in other countries. There is no example of any one that has died in it; and you may believe I am very well satisfied of the safety of this experiment, since I intend to try it on my dear little son.

I am patriot enough to take pains to bring this useful invention into fashion in England; and I should not fail to write to some of our doctors very particularly about it, if I knew any one of them that I thought had virtue enough to destroy such a considerable branch of their revenue for the good of mankind. But that distemper is too beneficial to them not to expose to all their resentment the hardy wight that should undertake to put an end to it. Perhaps, if I live to return, I may, however, have courage to war with them – *The Letters and Works of Lady Mary Wortley Montagu*, 1803.

A Surgeon Speaks

If I have any reputation I have earned it dearly for none ever endured more anxiety before an operation, yet from the time I began to operate all uneasiness ceased, and I have had better success than some others. I do not impute it to more knowledge but to the happiness of a mind that was never ruffled or disconcerted, and a hand that never trembled during any operation – William Cheselden, 1727.

Buggs must be Destroyed, *c*. 1750

Charles Harvey, Upholder,

At the George, in Coventry-Court, near St. James's, Haymarket, *Sells* the Famous Remedy for Destroying *Buggs*. Two Quart Bottles fill'd for 3s. 6d. with printed Directions, and undertakes to clean Beds and Houses of these most nauseous Vermin. I can refer to Gentry and others in most Parts of the Town, where I have done their Beds and Houses, for the Truth of my Assertion. This Remedy hath no ill Scent nor in any ways prejudicial to the Furniture.

More Particulars may be seen in my framed Bills in the Walks of the Royal Exchange, and at most Coffee-houses of Note.

N.B. I make all Sorts of Furniture in the genteelest Taste, buy, sell, and appraise all sorts of Household Goods, for ready Money only, and perform Funerals in the compleatest Manner.

The Golden Elixir of Life, *c*. 1750

The most excellent Imperial Golden Elixir of Life is Prepared and Sold by the Widow of the Hon. Major *Henry Poquet*.

Which said Elixir, for its extraordinary Virtues, surpasses all ever made : it's of great Effect against the Gout, it cures Rheumatism, Scurvy, Green-Sickness, and Worms; also eradicates all Obstructions of the Liver, and the Gripings and Twistings of the Guts. It is an effectual cure for Coughs, Phlegms, and Nervous Disorders; and is a great Restorative of Life, and an entire Cure to False-Conceptions and Dropsical Humours; and exceedingly good for Painters, being used by their Trade to have the Dry Gripes, it being an effectual Cure. Their late Majesties King William III and King George; their late Serene Highnesses Prince Eugene, the Duke of Zell, and his Grace the late Duke of Marlborough, all took it with Success; and divers Persons of Distinction. It is of so innocent a nature, that young Children, and Women with Child, may take it with Safety, and Lying-In Women.

9 Work and Wages

Food, Wages, and the Cost of Living in Scotland

Their tables were as full as at present, tho' very ill dress'd and as ill served up. They eat out of Pewder, often ill cleaned; but were nicer in their linen than now, which was renewed every day in most Gentlemens familys, and allwise napkins besides the cloth. The servants eat

Fishermen and their wives near Inverness, *c.* 1725. 'The women tuck up their garments to an indecent height and wade to the vessels . . . they take the fishermen upon their backs and bring them on shore in the same manner.'

ill; having a sett form for the week, of three days broth and salt meat, the rest megare, with plenty of bread and small beer. Their wages were small till the Vails [customary fees from the master or his guests] were abolished; the men from 3 to 4 pounds in the year, the maids from 30 shillings to 40. At those times I mention few of the maids could either sew or dress linen; it was all smouthed in the mangle but the Lady's headdresses, which were done by their own maids, and the gentlemen's shirts by the housekeeper. They in general employed as many servants as they do at present in the country but not in the towns; for one man servant was thought sufitient for most familys, or two at most, unless they keept a Carrage, which was a thing very uncommon in those days, and only used by the Nobles of great fortune. The prices of provisions were about a third of what they are now; beef from 1½ to 2 pen. per pound; Butter 2 pce ½ peny; Cheese 3 fardings or 1 peny; eggs 1 p. the Dozen; Veal 5 shillings the whole; a hen 4 pence; Geese and Turkies 1 shilling. Nether was the provisions much raised till after the Rebellion in the fortyfive, when riches increased considerably — Elizabeth Mure, *Some Observations of the Change of Manners in My Own Time*, 1700-1790.

Textiles in East Anglia

An eminent weaver of Norwich gave me a scheme of their trade on this occasion, by which, calculating from the number of looms at that time employed in the city of Norwich only, besides those employed in other towns in the same country, he made it appear very plain, that there were 120,000 people employed in the woollen and silk and wool manufactures of that city only, not that the people all lived in the city, tho' Norwich is a very large and populous city too. But I say, they were employed for spinning the yarn used for such goods as were all made in that city. . . .

This shows the wonderful extent of the Norwich manufacture, or stuff-weaving trade, by which so many thousands of families are maintained. Their trade indeed felt a very sensible decay, and the cries of the poor began to be very loud, when the wearing of painted calicoes was grown to such an height in England, as was seen about two or three years ago; but an Act of Parliament having been obtained, though not without great struggle, in the years 1720, and 1721, for prohibiting the use and wearing of calicoes, the stuff trade revived incredibly;

Apprentices at their silk looms in Spitalfields, *c*. 1747. From an engraving by William Hogarth representing Industry and Idleness. Here we see the idle and industrious apprentices at work while their master is watching them from the doorway.

Spitalfields had been the centre of the London silk trade since the coming of the French Protestant refugees after the revocation of the Edict of Nantes, 1685.

and as I passed this part of the country in the year 1723, the manufacturers assured me that there was not in all the eastern and middle part of Norfolk any hand, unemployed, if they would work; and that the very children after four or five years of age, could every one earn their own bread – Daniel Defoe, *A Tour Through the Whole Island of Great Britain*, 1726.

Wages of Farm Servants in Scotland

About 1730 our best ploughmen had only forty shillings a-year, besides *bounties – i.e.*, certain articles of apparel manufactured in the family, which amounted to a third of the wages. The *little* man [young man learning to plough] had about £11 Scots [18s. 4d. sterling], the *pleghan* [farm boy] £5 or £6, and the maid-servants £8 exclusive of the *bounties*. But about fifty years ago the servants entered into a combination to raise their wages. The epithets given to the ringleaders are still remembered by old people, and one of them, *Windy* Shaw, is still alive. Their demands at that time were, however, very moderate, being only £4 Scots of addition to the *big* man [principal ploughman], and to the other servants in proportion. But in 1760, after several small rises, the ploughman's wages did not exceed £3 sterling, and the women's were about 20s. a year.

We shall specify the bounties paid to the different servants. The *big* man had 5 eln [ells] of *grey*, and if he stayed a second year, as much black kelt or finer *grey* stuff, 2 harn [coarse linen] shirts, 2 pair of shoes, and 2 pair *plaiding* [woollen] hose. The *little* man had 3 or 4 elms of grey according to his size. The women a serge or drugget gown, 2 harn shirts, an apron, 2 pair shoes, and 2 pair stockings. The clothes were all made at the master's expense — John Ramsay, *Scotland and Scotsmen in the Eighteenth Century*.

Bricklayer's Bill

Mr William Blakeway's Bill of Materials had, and of Work done by Thomas Halling, Bricklayer, 5 June 1732.

	£.	s.	d.
For 8,000 of bricks at 12s. per M. [thousand]	4	16	0
,, 4,000 of tiles at 20.	4	0	0
,, 15 hundred of lime at 12s. 6d. per hundred	9	7	6
,, 14 load of sand at 2s. 6d. per load	1	15	0
,, 500 nine-inch paving tiles at 11s. per hundred	2	15	0
,, 30 ridge tiles at 1½d. per piece	0	4	4½
,, 3 weeks and 2 days work for myself at 3s. per diem	3	0	0
,, 25 days work and a half for my man at 2s. 6d. per diem	3	3	9
,, a labourer, 25 days work and a half at 1s. 8d. per diem	1	18	0
Their sum total is	30	12	5½

The Making of a Watch

The use of 'engines' had reduced the expense of workmanship to a trifle in comparison with what it was before and brought the work to such an exactness that no hand can imitate it. The movement-maker forges his wheels and turns them to the just dimensions, sends them to the cutter and has them cut at a trifling expense. He has nothing to do when he takes them from the cutter but to finish them and turn the corners of the teeth. The pinions made of steel are drawn at the mill so that the watchmaker has only to file down the points and fix them to the proper wheels. The springs are made by a tradesman who does nothing else, and the chains by another. These last are frequently made by women. . . . There are workmen who make nothing else but the caps and studs for watches. . . . After the watchmaker has got home all the . . . parts of which it consists he gives the whole to the finisher, having first had the brass wheels gilded by the gilder, and adjusts it to the proper time. The watchmaker puts his name on the plate and is esteemed the maker, though he has not made in his shop the smallest wheel belonging to it. It is supposed, however, that he can make all the movements, and apprentices are still learned to cut them by hand. He must be a judge of the goodness of the work at first sight, and put his name to nothing but what will stand the severest trial for the price of the watch depends upon the reputation of the maker only – R. Campbell, *The London Tradesmen*, 1747.

Cottage industry in the eighteenth century. Most cottages had a spinning wheel. The old woman is winding yarn into skeins for weaving.

Marine chronometer, 1736, by John Harrison. The Board of Longitude offered monetary reward for an accurate means of determining longitude at sea. Between 1728 and 1769 Harrison submitted no less than 4 chronometers to the Board who took 40 years before saying they were satisfied and rewarding him. His chronometer kept exact time independent of the motion of the ship, variations of heat, cold, wet, dry. Comparing time with local time at any place made it easy to find difference in longitude.

10 Trade and Money

The Way the Silk-Weaver's Trade was Recruited

In the first place few masters take apprentices, and when they do, seldom more than one, and perhaps a son or near relation. Secondly, as to the journeymen, the essence of the charge is false . . . for where there is one that has money with an apprentice there are fifty that have none at all, and the most they have, when they can get it, is not above £5 or £6, and the reason of this proves itself. For in the first place they commonly take such poor boys apprentices as have been first brought up to the trade, for you must know that every workman has a boy to attend to him, to help him pick his silk clean, to fill his quills, and in a flowered work to draw up the figure. Some of these things these boys are able to do at the age of six or seven, for which they receive 2s., 3s., 4s., and 4s. 6d. a week, which is a great help to their poor fathers and mothers. This they continue till fourteen, at which time they seek for a master and masters also seek for such boys. Secondly, it is of much more advantage to a master to take such a boy without money, than a stranger with money, and the parents of such boys being very poor, 'tis ridiculous to say they are taken for the sake of the money – *The Just Complaints of the Poor Weavers*, 1719.

Great Trade

The quantity of herrings that are catched in this season are diversely accounted for; some have said, that the towns of Yarmouth and Lowestoft only, have taken forty thousand last [last is twelve barrels] in a season; I will not venture to confirm that report; but this I have heard the merchants themselves say, (viz) That they have cured, that is to say, hanged and dried in the smoke, 40,000 barrels of merchantable redherrings in one season, which is in itself (though far short of the other) yet a very considerable article; and it is to be added, that this is besides all the herrings consumed in the country towns of both those populous counties, for thirty miles from the sea, whither very great quantities are carried every tide during the whole season.

But this is only one branch of the great trade carried on in this town [Yarmouth]. Another part of this commerce, is in the exporting these herrings after they are cured; and for this their merchants have a great trade to Genoa, Leghorn, Naples, Messina, and Venice; as also to Spain and Portugal, also exporting with their herring very great quantities of worsted stuffs, and stuffs made of silk and worsted, camblets [mixed cloth], &c. the manufactures of the neighbouring city of Norwich, and the places adjacent.

Besides this; they carry on a very considerable trade with Holland, whose opposite neighbours they are; and a vast quantity of woollen manufactures they export to the Dutch every year. Also they have a fishing trade to the north-seas for white fish, which from the place are called the North-Sea cod.

They have also a considerable trade to Norway, and to the Baltic, from whence they bring back deals, and fir-timber, oaken plank, baulks, spars, oars, pitch, tar, hemp, flax, spruce, canvas, and sail-cloth; with all manner of naval stores, which they generally have a consumption for in their own part, where they build a very great number of ships every year, besides re-fitting and repairing the old.

Add to this the coal trade between Newcastle and the river of the Thames, in which they are so improved of late years, that they have now a greater share of it than any other town in England; and have quite worked the Ipswich men out of it, who had formerly the chief share of the colliery in their hands — Daniel Defoe, *A Tour Through the Whole Island of Great Britain*, 1726.

Some Particular Trade

But the neighbourhood of London, which sucks the vitals of trade in this island to itself, is the chief reason of any decay of business in this place [Ipswich], and I shall in the course of these observations, hint at it, where many good sea-ports and large towns, though farther off than Ipswich, and as well fitted for commerce, are yet swallowed up by the immense indraft of trade to the city of London; and more decayed beyond all comparison, than Ipswich is supposed to be; as Southampton, Weymouth, Dartmouth, and several others which I shall speak to in their order. And if it be otherwise at this time, with some other towns, which are lately increased in trade and navigation, wealth, and people, while their neighbours decay, it is because they have some particular trade or accident to trade, which is a kind of nostrum to them, inseparable to the place, and which fixes there by the nature of the thing; as the herring-fishery to Yarmouth; the coal trade to Newcastle; the Leeds clothing-trade; the export of butter and lead, and the great corn trade for Holland, is to Hull; the Virginia and West-India trade at Liverpool, the Irish trade at Bristol, and the like. Thus the war has brought a flux of business and people, and consequently of wealth, to several places, as well as to Portsmouth, Chatham, Plymouth, Falmouth, and others; and were any wars like those, to continue 20 years with the Dutch, or any nation whose fleets lay that way, as the Dutch do, it would be the like perhaps at Ipswich in a few years, and at other places on the same coast — Daniel Defoe, *A Tour Through the Whole Island of Great Britain*, 1726.

Trade and Wealth

Upon the whole, to sum it up in a few words Trade is the Wealth of the World; Trade makes the Difference as to Rich and Poor, between one Nation and another; Trade nourishes Industry, Industry begets Trade; Trade dispenses the natural Wealth of the World, and Trade raises new Species of Wealth, which Nature knew nothing of; Trade has two Daughters, whose fruitful Progeny in Arts may be said to employ Mankind; namely Manufacture and Navigation — Daniel Defoe, 1728.

11 The Poor

Reactionary Comment on Attempts to Reduce Poverty

Increase of trade, and wealth, having produced an increase of luxury, and made the necessaries of life more expensive, it is proper that wages should be increased: but not yet beyond the bounds of proportion; for it will be found in those manufacturing occupations, in which labourers get the most money, they are the most disorderly, continually combining together to leave their work, unless their masters consent to increase their wages, and which only proves a temporary compromise, till they have an opportunity of making a further demand. On the contrary, where less wages are given, we shall find the people more happy, and contented, their wives more attended to, and their children brought up with more religion, and better morals – from *The Times*.

The Miserable Condition of Ireland

Swift, in a letter to the Earl of Peterborough on 28 April 1726, sets out the grievances of Ireland.

'*My Lord*,
... First, that all persons born in Ireland are called and treated as Irishmen, although their fathers and grandfathers were born in England; and their predecessors having been conquerors of Ireland, it is humbly conceived they ought to be on as good a foot as any subjects of Britain, according to the practice of all other nations, and particularly of the Greeks and Romans.

Secondly, that they are denied the natural liberty of exporting their manufactures to any country which is not engaged in a war with England.

Thirdly, that whereas there is a University in Ireland, founded by Queen Elizabeth, where youth are instructed with a much stricter discipline than either in Oxford or Cambridge, it lies under the greatest discouragements, by filling all the principal employments, civil and ecclesiastical, with persons from England, who have neither interest, property, acquaintance, nor alliance, in that kingdom; contrary to the practice of all other States in Europe which are governed by viceroys, at least what hath never been used without the utmost discontents of the people.

Fourthly, that several of the bishops sent over to Ireland, having been clergymen of obscure condition, and without other distinction than that of chaplains to the governors, do frequently invite over their old acquaintances or kindred, to whom they bestow the best preferment in their gift. The like may be said of the judges, who take with them one or two dependents, to whom they give their countenance; and who, consequently, without other merit, grow immediately into the chief business of their courts. The same practice is followed by all others in civil employment, if they have a cousin, a valet, or a footman in their family, born in England.

Fifthly, that all civil employments, grantable in reversion, are given to persons who reside in England.

The people of Ireland, who are certainly the most loyal subjects in the world, cannot but conceive that most of these hardships have been the consequence of some unfortunate representations, at least, in former times; and the whole body of the gentry feel the effects in a very sensible part, being utterly destitute of all means to make provision for their younger sons, either in the Church, the law, the revenue, or, of late, in the army; and in the desperate condition of trade, it is equally vain to think of making them merchants. All they have left is, at the expiration of leases, to rack their tenants, which they have done to such a degree, that there is not one farmer in a hundred through the kingdom who can afford shoes or stockings to his children, or to eat flesh, or drink anything better than sour milk or water, twice in a year; so that the whole country, except the Scottish plantation in the north, is a scene of misery and desolation hardly to be matched on this side of Lapland.

...I think it manifest, that whatever circumstances can possibly contribute to make a country poor and despicable, are all united with respect to Ireland. The nation controlled by laws to which they do not consent, disowned by their brethren and countrymen, refused the liberty not only of trading with their own manufacturers, but even their native commodities, forced to seek for justice many hundred miles by sea and land, rendered in a manner incapable of serving their king and country in any employment of honour, trust, or profit; and all this without the least demerit; while the governors sent over thither can possibly have no affection to the people, further than what is instilled into them by their own justice and love of mankind, which do not always operate; and whatever they please to represent hither is never called in question – *correspondence of Jonathan Swift*, edited by F. Elrington Ball.

The Benefits of Workhouses

It is hoped that workhouses would effectually cure a very bad practice in parish officers, who, to save expense, are apt to ruin children by putting them out as early as they can to any sorry master that will take them, without any concern for their education and welfare, on account of the little money that is given with them. However, there will be this one good effect from workhouses thus regulated, that the next generation of persons in town will be made better and the children of the poor, instead of being bred up in irreligion and vice to an idle vagabond life, will have the fear of God before their eyes, get habits of virtue, be inured to labour, and thus become useful to their country – *Account of Several Workhouses*, 1732.

The Poor of London

That the poor are a very great burden, and even a nuisance to this kingdom; that the laws for relieving their distresses, and restraining their vices, have not answered those purposes; and that they are at present very ill provided for, and much worse governed, are truths which every man, I believe, will acknowledge. Such have been the unanimous complaints of all the writers who have considered this matter down from the days of Queen Elizabeth; such is apparently the sense of our present legislature; and such is the universal voice of the nation.

The facts must be very glaring that can produce this unanimous concurrence in opinion; and so in truth they are. Every man who hath any property must feel the weight of that tax which is levied for the use of the poor; and every man who hath any understanding must see how absurdly it is applied. So very useless indeed is this heavy tax, and so wretched its disposition, that it is a question whether the poor or the rich are actually more dissatisfied, or have indeed greater reason to be dissatisfied; since the plunder of the one serves so little to the real advantage of the other; for while a million yearly is raised among the former many of the latter are starved; many more languish in want and misery; of the rest numbers are found begging or pilfering in the streets to-day, and to-morrow are locked up in goals and bridewells.

Of all these deplorable evils we have constant evidence before our eyes. The sufferings of the poor are, indeed, less observed than their misdeeds; not from any want of compassion, but because they are less known; and this is the true reason why we so often hear them mentioned with abhorrence, and so seldom with pity. But if we were to make a progress through the outskirts of this town, and look into the habitations of the poor, we should there behold such pictures of human misery as must move the compassion of every heart that deserves the name of human. What, indeed, must be his composition who could see whole families in want of every necessary of life, oppressed with hunger, cold, nakedness, and filth; and with diseases, the certain consequences of all these — what, I say, must be his composition who could look into such a scene as this, and be affected only in his nostrils.

That such wretchedness as this is so little lamented, arises therefore from its being so little known; but, if this be the case with the sufferings of the poor, it is not so with their misdeeds. They starve, and freeze, and rot among themselves; but they beg, and steal, and rob among their betters. There is not a parish in the Liberty of Westminster which doth not raise thousands annually for the poor, and there is not a street in that Liberty which doth not swarm all day with beggars, and all night with thieves. Stop your coach at what shop you will, however expeditious the tradesman is to attend you, a beggar is commonly beforehand with him; and if you should not directly face his door the tradesman must often turn his head while you are talking to him, or the same beggar, or some other thief at hand, will pay a visit to his shop! I omit to speak of the more open and violent insults which are every day committed on His Majesty's subjects in the streets and highways. They are enough known and enough spoken of. The depredations on property are less noticed, particularly those in the parishes within ten miles of London. To these every man is not obnoxious, and therefore it is not every man's business to suppress them. These are, however, grown to the most deplorable height; insomuch that the gentleman is daily, or rather nightly, plundered of his pleasure, and the farmer of his livelihood — Henry Fielding, *A Proposal for Making an Effectual Provision for the Poor*, 1753.

12 Agriculture

Turnips for Cattle and Sheep

This part of England [Suffolk] is also remarkable for being the first where the feeding and fattening of cattle, both sheep as well as black cattle with turnips, was first practised in England, which is made a very great part of the improvement of their lands to this day; and from whence the practice is spread over most of the east and south parts of England, to the great enriching of the farmers, and increase of fat cattle. And though some have objected against the goodness of the flesh thus fed with turnips, and have fancied it would taste of the root; yet upon experience 'tis found, that at market there is no difference nor can they that buy, single out one joint of mutton from another by the taste. So that the complaint which our nice palates at first made, begins to cease of itself; and a very great quantity of beef, and mutton also, is brought every year, and every week to London, from this side of England, and much more than was formerly known to be fed there — Daniel Defoe, *A Tour Through the Whole Island of Great Britain*, 1726.

Migratory Labour

. . . at the beginning of May there come from Ireland over to England a very large number of Irishmen who go and hire themselves every- where to the farmers. The whole of this part of England which lies immediately north and east of London, carries on nearly all its hay- making and harvesting work with only these people, who come over at the beginning of May and remain there the whole summer. . . . So it is the case with those from Wales that they earn their money also on this side of England in Kent, for towards the haymaking season, the folk come from thence in very large numbers down to the country parts of Kent to work for wages; but with this difference that instead of only men coming as from Ireland, there come mostly only women and girls from Wales, all well, cleanly and very neatly clad — P. Kalm, *Account of his visit to England on his way to America in 1748.*

13 Industry

Iron-Works in Sussex

All this part of the country is very agreeably pleasant, wholesome and
fruitful, I mean quite from Guildford to this place [Westerham in
Kent], and is accordingly overspread with good towns, gentlemen's
houses, populous villages, abundance of fruit, with hop-grounds and
cherry orchards, and the lands well cultivated; but all on the right-hand,
that is to say, south, is exceedingly grown with timber, has abundance
of waste, and wild grounds, and forests, and woods, with many large
iron-works, at which they cast great quantities of iron caldrons,
chimney-backs, furnaces, retorts, boiling pots, and all such necessary
things of iron; besides iron cannon, bomb-shells, stink-pots [hand-
missiles giving off suffocating smoke, used boarding a ship], hand-
grenadoes, and cannon ball, etc., in an infinite quantity, and which
turn to very great account; tho' at the same time the works are prodigiously expensive, and the quantity of wood they consume is exceeding great, which keeps up that complaint I mentioned before, that
timber would grow scarce, and consequently dear, from the great
quantity consumed in the iron-works in Sussex — Daniel Defoe, *A Tour
through the Whole Island of Great Britain*, 1726.

A Coal Pit at Ashby de la Zouch

September 7, 1728. I have nothing very remarkable to tell you except
that at Ashby de la Zouch in Leicestershire I ventured down into a
coal pit between 200 and 300 feet deep. It was very safe going down.
The way is a fellow gets upon a rope and ties himself fast and then
ye person yt goes down sets [sits] in his lap. When I was down I could
not stand upright so yt I could not go very far in it. There are horses
which have been down there for 8 or 10 years and never once come up
in all yt time. The cole mine yt I was in belongs to one Mrs Wilkins who

goes down herself very often and dines there and spends the whole day there. It was so very wet that I came up like a drowned rat. The only remarkable places yt I have been at since are Litchfield and Shrewsbury — Earl Cowper to his elder sister, Lady Sarah, in London.

The Works at Coalbrookdale

... Methinks how delightful it would be to walk with thee into fields and woods, then to go into the Dale to view the works; the stupendous Bellows whose alternate roars, like the foaming billows, is awful to hear; the mighty Cylinders, the wheels that carry on so many different Branches of the work, is curious to observe; the many other things which I cannot ennumerate; but if thou wilt but come, I am sure thou would like it. It's really pleasant about our house, and so many comes and goes that we forget it's the Country till we look out at the window and see the woodland prospect — Hannah Darby, Abraham's daughter, to her aunt, Rachel Thompson, 1753.

The Worsley-Manchester Canal: Barton Aqueduct. From Arthur Young's *Six Months' Tour through the North of England*, 1770. Young describes the Worsley-Manchester Canal which was constructed by James Brindley, 1760-1. The canal was carried across the River Irwell at Barton Bridge by an aqueduct, seen here, as a barge is moving over it.

14 Religion

Quakers

I think that it is principally owing to the Presbyterian sect that Sunday is solemnised as it is in England. During the Commonwealth, Cromwell, who was a Presbyterian, severely forbade shows or amusements of any kind, as well as concerts and games. All these are still forbidden, and on Sundays you never hear the sound of music. There is no opera, no comedy, no sounds in the streets. Card-playing on this day is also strictly forbidden, at least for citizens and common people, for persons of rank, I believe, do not scruple to play. Unfortunately, a great number of the people divert themselves in the taverns, and there indulge in debauch.

The curious sect of Quakers, or Shakers, arose in the troubled times New England was torn by revolutions, anarchy, and fanaticism, that is to say in the time of Cromwell. A rather crazy shoemaker's apprentice, George Fox, was the founder of this sect. It can almost be said that the Quakers form a particular nation of people, quite different from ordinary English citizens, by their language, manner of dressing, and religion.

Amongst their other customs, one of which is the use of the pronoun 'thou', is that of never giving any man his titles, whatever his position or worth may be, for everyone to them is but a vile earthworm inhabiting this planet for a few years. Quakers make use of a sort of Bible talk, which strikes you more particularly, as it appears to date two hundred years back, no Bible having been printed in England in the fine modern language, the earliest edition of the Holy Book being still in use.

The Quakers' mode of dressing is as curious as is their language; the men wear large, unlooped, flapping hats, without buttons or loops; their coats are as plain as possible, with no pleatings or trimmings, and no buttons or button-holes on the sleeves, pockets, or waists. If any brother were to wear ruffles to his shirts or powder on his hair, he would be considered impious. The most austere and zealous do not even wear shoe-buckles, but tie their shoes with cords. The women wear no ribbons, no lace, their gowns being of one modest colour, without hoops, and their caps have no frills or pleatings, and are of a peculiar shape, made of silk, and worn pleated on the forehead in a certain fashion particular to them. It must be owned, in truth, that this simple and modest attire suits many of these women admirably. Quakers' clothes, though of the simplest and plainest cut, are of excellent quality; their hats, clothes, and linen are of the finest, and so are the silken tissues the women wear. These people call each other 'brother' and 'sister', and to persons who are not of their sect they give the name of 'friend'; they never make any compliments, and do not salute by taking off their hats or by making a curtsey.

All Quakers are merchants, and they never charge more for their goods than their worth. One day a young dandy, desirous of purchasing cloth for a coat, went into a Quaker's shop in London, and, seeing some cloth that suited his taste, he commenced haggling over the price of the merchandise. Finding that the Quaker would take nothing off the price of this article, the young man swore an oath that he would not buy it at the price. At this the tradesman without a word folded up the cloth and put it away. The dandy proceeded to try various shops, but finding no cloth to suit him as well, either for price, colour, or quality, as what he had first seen, he returned and asked for the cloth. The Quaker answered quietly, 'Friend, thou didst swear thou wouldst not purchase my cloth at the price; as I can taking nothing off, I cannot sell it thee, else I should be guilty of making thee swear a false oath; go and buy thy cloth elsewhere.' Few merchants, I think, would have had the delicacy of feeling this Quaker merchant had.

Quakers claim to be Christians after the manner of the early members of the Church, but I do not know whether this appellation can really be given them, for they are never baptized. When a child is born the father or a near relative takes it up in his arms and says, 'Welcome to this vale of misery.' They declare they have communion with God, not with the lips but with the heart, and that communion was instituted to remind men of our Saviour's death, and that they, having His memory constantly before them, have no need of a reminder. Quakers have neither priests nor ministers, for they say it is not right that men should choose their own preachers. They are what we call inspired, and they consider themselves as machines made to move, act, and think by a Divine Providence.

I have attended some of their conventional assemblies. The meeting remains wrapped in profound silence, sometimes for as much as half' an hour. The men's faces are hidden in the borders of their wide, flapping hats, which they never remove, and the women draw down their pretty silken caps, or hide their faces with their fans. Everyone seems plunged in deep meditation, interrupted from time to time by a deep-drawn sigh, a groan, or a sob from some member of the assembly. Quakers also show their emotion by being taken with shaking fits, which make them appear to be suffering from fever, this latter characteristic being the origin of the name Quaker. Silence is at last suddenly interrupted by a brother jumping up, exclaiming, 'The Spirit moves me.' He repeats this phrase thrice, and then addresses his brethren in an incomprehensible jargon, repeating several times running those phrases he thinks most effective, and this is what this sect call preaching the gospel. When the first Quaker has finished his discourse another will rise in his stead, and sometimes several men and women will insist on being heard, declaring that they must speak, being inspired. These addresses are usually absurd; things worth listening to being intermingled with many that are not. This sect of Quakers tends to diminish every day, for amongst them are many brethren anxious to taste of the honours of this life, and many youthful Quakers, whose fathers have died leaving them rich, have a longing to wear buttons on their sleeves and ruffles to their shirts, and to live after the fashion of other young men – César de Saussure, *A Foreign View of England in the Reigns of George I and George II*, 1725-9.

The Dissenters' Plea

The Dissenters state their case, solved later by Indemnity Act, annually after 1727. The Dissenters' plea for asking this favour of the Parliament [the repeal of the Test and Corporation Acts] seemed very natural and reasonable; they said they had for above forty years shown themselves steady friends to the constitution of England in the State, and constant supporters of the established government on Revolution principles; they had served hitherto without any reward, and now desired no other gratuity than the bare removal of that unjust distinction made between them and the rest of their fellow-subjects under which they had so long laboured and by which they were excluded from all employments of trust or profit. They said what made this request more reasonable was, that the hardship they now complained of had never been laid upon them all, had they not originally consented to it themselves, and that the reason of their consenting to it had been merely for the public and the common Protestant cause; circumstances at that time requiring their voluntary submission to this self-denial act in order to facilitate the exclusion of Papists from all places of power when this kingdom was on the brink of being subjected to their sway under the authority of a Popish successor. They further added that they had not only always shown themselves unwavering and indefatigable champions for the Protestant succession, but that they had equally proved themselves firm and constant friends to what was called the Whig party, and the set of men now in power; consequently, if they could not get rid of this stigmatizing brand of reproach that declared them unfit to be trusted with any employment in the executive part of the civil government under a Whig Parliament, they could never hope for relief at all, since the other set of men, who called themselves the Church party, and whom they had always opposed, should they come into power, would not only from principle forbear to show the Dissenters any favour, but would certainly from resentment go still further, and probably load them with some new oppression. . . .

. . . This design of the Presbyterians put the Administration under great difficulties and into great apprehensions; they saw the injustice of opposing their petitions if it came into Parliament, and the danger there was, on the other hand, of showing it any countenance; they knew it would seem the last ingratitude in any who called themselves Whigs to reject it, and the highest imprudence to receive it; for though the clergy had hitherto been kept pretty quiet by nothing being attempted either to restrain their power or to favour their adversaries, yet the ministers were sure that if any step was taken that looked like encouragement to the Dissenters, it would inevitably turn all the parsons, to a man, in the approaching elections, against every one that should appear to forward it, and as to those who did not forward it, the [Dissenting] ministers would never give them a vote again — Lord Hervey, *Memoirs of the Reign of George II*.

Why Daughters Fail in Life of Devotion

Matilda is a fine woman, of good breeding, great sense, and much religion. She has three daughters that are educated by herself. She will not trust them with any one else, or at any school, for fear they should learn anything ill. She stays with the dancing-master all the time he is with them, because she will hear everything that is said to them. She has heard them read the Scriptures so often, that they can repeat great part of it without book: and there is scarce a good book of devotion, but you may find it in their closets.

Had Matilda lived in the first ages of Christianity, when it was practised in the fulness and plainness of its doctrines, she had in all probability been one of its greatest saints. But as she was born in corrupt times, where she wants examples of Christian perfection, and hardly ever saw a piety higher than her own; so she has many defects, and communicates them all to her daughters.

Matilda never was meanly dressed in her life; and nothing pleases her in dress, but that which is very rich and beautiful to the eye.

Her daughters see her great zeal for religion, but they see an equal earnestness for all sorts of finery. They see she is not negligent of her devotion, but then they see her more careful to preserve her complexion, and to prevent those changes which time and age threaten her with.

They are afraid to meet her, if they have missed the church; but then they are more afraid to see her, if they are not laced as strait as they can possibly be.

She often shows them her own picture, which was taken when their father fell in love with her. She tells them how distracted he was with passion at the first sight of her, and that she had never had so fine a complexion, but for the diligence of her good mother, who took exceeding care of it.

Matilda is so intent upon all the arts of improving their dress, that she has some new fancy almost every day, and leaves no ornament untried, from the richest jewel to the poorest flower. She is so nice and critical in her judgement, so sensible of the smallest error, that the maid is often forced to dress and undress her daughters three or four times a day, before she can be satisfied with it.

As to the patching, she reserves that to herself, for, she says, if they are not stuck on with judgement, they are rather a prejudice than an advantage to the face.

The children see so plainly the temper of their mother, that they even affect to be more pleased with dress, and to be more fond of every little ornament than they really are, merely to gain her favour — William Law, *A Serious Call to a Devout and Holy Life*, 1729.

Patronage

The patronage of the lord of the manor still controlled 'livings' in the Church.

My Lord,

We presume that you are acquainted with the Death of our late Incumbent, the Revd. Mr. Richard Worrel; and understanding that your lordship hath reserved to your self the Presentation of Wasen, We, whose names are underwritten — your lordship's Ancient Tenants and Inhabitants of the said Parish — do with all humility beseech your lordship to present the said Living to the Revd. Anthony Thompson, who is now Chaplain to the Rt. Hon. Earl Waldegrave, now at Paris with him. He is a Gentleman of an undoubted Character, and can be handsomely recommended to your lordship and is well-known to us from his youth. If your lordship please to grant this favour his Spouse will send for him over. This condescension of your lordship will be for ever acknowledged with the utmost gratitude by your lordship's most obliged and obedient servants,   *Robert Loveday*

                                     Wm. Buttons — his marke

                                     Benj. Buttons

1732   *Thomas Humfrey*

Choosing a Chaplain

When Dukes or noble Lords a Chaplain hire,
They first of his Capacities enquire.
If stoutly qualified to drink and smoke,
If not too nice to bear an impious Joke,
If tame enough to be the common Jest,
This is a Chaplain to his Lordship's Taste.

R. Dodsley, *The Art of Preaching*, 1738.

Methodism Begins

Fri. 19. I rode once more to Pensford, at the earnest request of several serious people. The place where they desired me to preach, was a little green spot near the town. But I had no sooner begun, than a great company of rabble, hired (as we afterwards found) for that purpose, came furiously upon us, bringing a bull which they had been baiting, and now strove to drive in among the people; but the beast was wiser than his drivers, and continually ran either on one side of us or the other, while we quietly sang praise to God, and prayed for about an hour. The poor wretches finding themselves disappointed, at length seized upon the bull, now weak and tired, after being so long torn and beaten both by dogs and men, and by main strength partly dragged and partly thrust him in among the people. When they had forced their way to the little table on which I stood, they strove several times to throw it down, by thrusting the helpless beast against it who of himself stirred no more than a log of wood. I once or twice put aside his head with my hand, that the blood might not drop upon my clothes, intending to go on as soon as the hurry should be a little over; but the table falling down, some of our friends caught me in their arms, and carried me right away on their shoulders, while the rabble wreaked their vengeance on the table, which they tore bit from bit. We went a little way off, where I finished my discourse without any noise or interruption.

Sun. 30. At seven, I walked down to Sand-Gate, the poorest and most contemptible part of the town, and standing at the end of the street with John Taylor, began to sing the hundredth psalm. Three or four people came out to see what was the matter, who soon increased to four or five hundred. I suppose there might be twelve or fifteen hundred before I had done preaching; to whom I applied these solemn words, 'He was wounded for our transgressions, he was bruised for our iniquities; the chastisement of our peace was upon him, and by his stripes we are healed.'

Observing the people when I had done to stand gaping and staring upon me, with the most profound astonishment, I told them, 'If you desire to know who I am, my name is John Wesley; at five in the evening, with God's help, I design to preach here again.'

At five, the hill on which I designed to preach was covered from the top to the bottom. I never saw so large a number of people together, either in Moorfields or at Kennington-Common. I knew it was not possible for the one-half to hear, although my voice was then strong and clear, and I stood so as to have them all in view, as they were ranged on the side of the hill. The word of God which I set before them was, 'I will heal their backsliding, I will love them freely.' After preaching, the poor people were ready to tread me under foot, out of pure love and kindness. I was some time before I could possibly get out of the press. I then went back another way than I came. But several were got to our inn before me; by whom I was vehemently importuned to stay with them, at least a few days, or, however, one day more. But I could not consent; having given my word to be at Birstal, with God's leave, on Tuesday night.

I was writing at Francis Ward's in the afternoon, when the cry arose, that 'the mob had beset the house.' We prayed that God would disperse them: and it was so; one went this way, and another that; so that, in half an hour, not a man was left. I told our brethren, 'Now is the time for us to go'; but they pressed me exceedingly to stay. So, that I might not offend them, I sat down, though I foresaw what would follow. Before five the mob surrounded the house again, in greater numbers than ever. The cry of one and all was, 'Bring out the Minister; we will have the Minister.' I desired one, to take their captain by the hand and bring him into the house. After a few sentences interchanged between us, the lion was become a lamb. I desired him to go and bring one or two more of the most angry of his companions. He brought in two, who were ready to swallow the ground with rage; but in two minutes they were as calm as he. I then bade them make way, that I might go out among the people. As soon as I was in the midst of them, I called for a chair, and standing up, asked. 'What do you want with me?' Some said, 'We want you to go with us to the Justice!' I replied, 'That I will with all my heart.' I then spoke a few words, which God applied; so that they cried out with might and main, 'The gentleman is an honest gentleman, and we will spill our blood in his defence.' I asked, 'Shall we go to the Justice to-night or in the morning?' Most of them cried, 'To-night, to-night': on which I went before, and two or three hundred followed; the rest returning whence they came.

The night came on before we had walked a mile, together with heavy rain. However, on we went to Bentley-Hall, two miles from Wednesbury. One or two ran before to tell Mr. Lane, 'They had brought Mr. Wesley before his worship.' Mr. Lane replied, 'What have I to do with Mr. Wesley? Go and carry him back again.' By this time the main body came up, and began knocking at the door. A servant told them, 'Mr. Lane was in bed.' His son followed, and asked, 'What was the matter?' One replied, 'Why, an't please you, they sing psalms all day; nay, and make folks rise at five in the morning; and what would your worship advise us to do?' 'To go home,' said Mr. Lane, 'and be quiet.'

Here they were at a full stop, till one advised to go to Justice Persehouse at Walsal. All agreed to this. So we hastened on, and about seven came to his house; but Mr. P— likewise sent word, 'That he was in bed.' Now they were at a stand again; but at last they all thought it the wisest course to make the best of their way home. About fifty of them understood to convoy me; but we had not gone a hundred yards when the mob of Walsal came pouring in, like a flood, and bore down all before them. The Darlston mob made what defence they could; but they were weary as well we out-numbered; so that, in a short time, many being knocked down, the rest ran away, and left me in their hands.

To attempt speaking was in vain; for the noise on every side was like the roaring of the sea; so they dragged me along till we came to the town, where seeing the door of a large house open, I attempted to go in; but a man, catching me by the hair, pulled me back into the middle of the mob. They made no more stop till they had carried me through the main street, from one end of the town to the other. I continued speaking all the time to those within hearing, feeling no pain or weariness. At the west end of the town, seeing a door half open, I made toward it, and would have gone in; but a gentleman in the shop would not suffer me, saying, 'They would pull the house down to the ground.' However, I stood at the door, and asked, 'Are you willing to hear me speak?' Many cried out, 'No, no! knock his brains out; down with him; kill him at once.' Others said, 'Nay, but we will hear him first.' I began asking, 'What evil have I done? Which of you all have I wronged in word or deed?' and continued speaking for above a quarter of an hour, till my voice suddenly failed; then the floods began to lift up their voice again; many crying out, 'Bring him away; bring him away.'

In the meantime my strength and my voice returned, and I broke out aloud into prayer. And now the man who just before headed the mob, turned and said, 'Sir, I will spend my life for you: follow me, and not one soul here shall touch a hair of your head.' Two or three of his fellows confirmed his words, and got close to me immediately; at the same time the gentleman in the shop cried out, 'For shame, for shame; let him go.' An honest butcher, who was a little farther off, said, 'It was a shame they should do thus;' and pulled back four or five, one after another, who were running on the most fiercely. The people then, as if it had been by common consent, fell back to the right and left; while those three or four men took me between them, and carried me through them all. But on the bridge the mob rallied again; we, therefore, went on one side, over the Mill-dam, and thence through the meadows, till a little before ten God brought me safe to Wednesbury; having lost only one flap of my waistcoat, and a little skin from one of my hands — John Wesley, *Journal*, 1739-91.

15 Science

Moving Pictures

Mr. Pinkentham in order to divert and oblige the gentry and others of Greenwich, Deptford, Woolwich, Lee and other adjacent places thereabouts, has remov'd the most famous artificial and wonderful moving pictures that came from Germany, and was seen at the Duke of Marlborough's Head in Fleet Street, and is now to be seen at the Hospital Tavern in Greenwich — *advertisement, c.* 1710.

The Rage for Flying

There are characters who had rather amuse the world, at the hazard of their lives, for a slender and precarious pittance, than follow an honest calling for an easy subsistence. A small figure of a man, seemingly composed of spirit and gristle, appeared in October (1732) to entertain the town (of Derby) by sliding down a rope. One end of this was to be fixed at the top of All Saints' steeple, and the other at the bottom of St. Michael's, a horizontal distance of eighty yards, this formed an inclined plane, extremely steep. A breastplate of wood, with a groove to fit the rope, and his own equilibrium, were to be his security while sliding down upon his belly with his arms and legs extended. He could not be more than six or seven seconds in this airy journey, in which he fired a pistol and blew a trumpet. The velocity with which he flew raised a fire by friction, and a bold stream of smoke followed him. He performed this wonderful exploit three successive days, in each of which he descended twice and marched up once. The latter took him more than an hour, in which he exhibited many surprising achievements, as sitting unconcerned with his arms folded, lying across the rope upon his back, and then upon his belly and his hams, blowing the trumpet, swinging round, hanging by the chin, the hand, the toe. The rope being too long for art to tighten, he might be said to have danced upon the slack rope. Though he succeeded at Derby, yet, in exhibiting soon after at Shrewsbury, he fell and lost his life.

Feats of activity are sure to catch the younger part of the world. No amusement was seen but the rope; walls, posts, trees, and houses were mounted for the pleasure of flying down; if a straggling scaffold-pole could be found it was reared for the convenience of flying; nay, even cats, dogs, and things inanimate, were applied in a double sense, to the rope. . . .

The rage for flying had continued two years in full force; I caught that rage, but not being able to procure a rope, I and my companions laid hold of a scaffold-pole in the absence of the workmen, who were erecting a house in Amen Corner, south of All Saints'. We placed one end in the churchyard, and the other in the chamber-window, and flew over the wall. We soon made the pole as bright as a looking-glass, but reduced our raiment to rags. To this day I never pass the place without a glance at the window.

A few young men, adepts in the art of flying, procured the consent of Sir Nathaniel Curzon to perform at Kedleston for the amusement of the family. They fastened one end of the rope to the top of the hall, the other in the park; but the unlucky performer, instead of flying over the river, fell in, blasted his character, and instead of regaling upon beef and ale, the whole bevy sneaked off privately – William Hutton, *Life* and *History of Derby*.

Benjamin Franklin Writes to Peter Collinson about an Electric Kite

Philadelphia, Oct. 1st, 1752.

As frequent mention is made in the public papers from Europe of the success of the Philadelphia experiment for drawing the electric fire from clouds by means of pointed rods of iron erected on high buildings, etc., it may be agreeable to the curious to be informed that the same experiment has succeeded in Philadelphia, tho' made in a different and more easy manner, which any one may try, as follows:

Make a small cross of two light strips of cedar; the arms so long, as to reach to the four corners of a large thin silk handkerchief, when extended: tie the corners of the handkerchief to the extremities of the cross; so you have the body of a kite; which being properly accommo-dated with a tail, loop and string, will rise in the air like those made of paper; but this, being of silk, is fitter to bear the wet and wind of a thunder gust without tearing.

To the tip of the upright stick of the cross is to be fixed a very sharp-pointed wire, rising a foot or more above the wood. To the end of the twine next the hand, is to be tied a silk riband; and where the twine and silk join, a key may be fasten'd.

The kite is to be raised, when a thunder-gust appears to be coming on (which is very frequent in this country) and the person, who holds the string, must stand within a door, or window, or under some cover, so that the silk riband may not be wet; and care must be taken that the twine does not touch the frame of the door or window.

As soon as any of the thunder-clouds come over the kite, the pointed wire will draw the electric fire from them; and the kite, with all the twine, will be electrified; and the loose filaments of the twine will stand out every way, and be attracted by an approaching finger.

When the rain has wet the kite and twine, so that it can conduct the electric fire freely, you will find it stream out plentifully from the key on the approach of your knuckle.

At this key the phial may be charged; and from electric fire thus obtain'd spirits may be kindled, and all the other electrical experiments may be performed, which are usually done by the help of a rubbed glass globe or tube, and thereby the sameness of the electric matter with that of lightning completely demonstrated.

I was pleased to hear of the success of my experiments in France and that they there begin to erect points upon their buildings. We had before placed them upon our academy and state-house spires – from *Philosophical Transactions.*

16 Travel

Barges

They give this name in England to a sort of pleasure boat, at one end of which is a little room handsomely painted and covered, with a table in the middle and benches round it, and at the other end, seats for 8, 10, 12, 20, 30, or 40 rowers. There are very few persons of great quality but what have their barges, though they do not frequently make use of them. Their watermen wear a jacket of the same colour they give for their livery with a pretty large silver badge upon their arm, with the nobleman's coat of arms embossed upon it. These watermen have some privileges, but they have no wages and are not domestic servants. They live in their own houses with their families and earn their livelihood as they can. The Lord Mayor of London and the several companies have also their barges and are carried in them upon certain solemn occasions.

The day of his investiture, the Lord Mayor with all his aldermen and train goes to the riverside, where a dozen or more barges and galleys are waiting for them. The Lord Mayor's barge is magnificent; it is enriched with gilding, carving, and delicate paintings; it is decked with banners, streamers and flags, and is manned by forty oarsmen, all wearing a bright-hued livery and caps of black velvet. The other barges are handsomely decorated likewise, one of them having a band of excellent musicians on board. A great number of ordinary but well-decorated boats follow and make a charming flotilla, keeping in good time to the strains of music. The boats stop at the stairs or Quai of Westminster, where the procession forms and goes on foot to the Grand Hall of Westminster — M. Misson, *Memoirs and Observations*, 1719.

English Roads

I left Tunbridge, for the same reason that I give, why others should leave it, when they are in my condition; namely, that I found my money almost gone; and tho' I had bills of credit [written orders to draw money from certain men by prearrangement] to supply myself in the course of my intended journey; yet I had none there; so I came away, or as they call it there, I retir'd; and came to Lewes, through the deepest, dirtiest, but many ways the richest, and most profitable country in that part of England.

The timber I saw here was prodigious, as well in quantity as in bigness, and seem'd in some places to be suffer'd to grow; only because it was so far off of any navigation, that it was not worth cutting down and carrying away; in dry summers, indeed, a great deal is carry'd away to Maidstone, and other places on the Medway; and sometimes I have seen one tree on a carriage, which they call there a tug, drawn by two and twenty oxen, and even then, 'tis carry'd so little a way, and then thrown down, and left for other tugs to take up and carry on, that sometimes 'tis two or three year before it gets to Chatham; for if once the rains come in, it stirs no more that year, and sometimes a whole summer is not dry enough to make the roads passable: Here I had a sight, which indeed I never saw in any other part of England: Namely, that going to church at a country village, not far from Lewes, I saw an ancient lady, and a lady of very good quality, I assure you, drawn to church in her coach with six oxen; nor was it done in frolic or humour, but meer necessity, the way being so stiff and deep, that no horses could go in it. — Daniel Defoe, *A Tour through the Whole Island of Great Britain*, 1726.

Turnpikes

At these gates travellers were stopped and made to pay a 'toll'. This money was taken to pay for road repairs. As travellers used the roads why shouldn't they pay for the upkeep?

. . . These roads [in Essex] were formerly deep, in time of floods dangerous, and at other times, in winter, scarce passable; they are now so firm, so safe, so easy to travellers, and carriages as well as cattle, that no road in England can yet be said to equal them; this was first done by the help of a turnpike, set up by Act of Parliament, about the year 1697, at a village near Ingerstone. Since that, another turnpike, set up at the corner of the Dog Row, near Mile-end; with an additional one at Rumford, which is called a branch, and paying at one, passes the person

A Country Inn Yard, 1747, from an engraving by William Hogarth. The heavy coach is seen leaving the courtyard of the 'Angel'. The body of the coach is hung on leather straps (a forerunner of springs). The name *Centurion* on the sailor's handle suggests that he sailed round the world with George Anson, 1740-4.

thro' both. This I say, being set up since the other, completes the whole, and we are told, that as the first expires in a year or two, this last will be sufficient for the whole, which will be a great ease to the country. The first toll near Ingerstone, being the highest rated public toll in England; for they take 8d for every cart, 6d for every coach, and 12d for every wagon; and in proportion for droves of cattle. For single horsemen indeed, it is the same as others pay, viz. 1d per horse, and we are told, while this is doing, that the gentlemen of the county design to petition the Parliament, to have the Commissioners of the last Act, whose turnpike, as above, is at Mile-end and Rumford empowered to take other turnpikes, on the other most considerable roads, and so to undertake, and repair all the roads in the whole county, I mean all the considerable roads — Daniel Defoe, *A Tour Through the Whole Island of Great Britain*, 1726.

Wheels Clash

The hackney coaches in London are a great convenience. About one thousand of these vehicles are to be found day and night in the public places and principal streets of the city and town. Most of them, to tell the truth, are ugly and dirty. The driver is perched high up on a wooden seat, as elevated as the imperial of a coach. The body of the carriage is very badly balanced, so that when inside you are most cruelly shaken, the pavement being very uneven, and most of the horses excellent and fast trotters. A drive costs one shilling, provided you do not go further than a certain distance; other drives will cost two or sometimes three shillings, according to distance. The drivers often ask more than is their due, and this is the case especially when they have to do with foreigners. To avoid being cheated, you must take the number of the coach marked on the door, and offer the driver a handful of coins, telling him to take his fare out of it. In this fashion of dealing he will not take more than his due, for should he do so you have a right to go and complain at the coach office, and the driver will be punished by being made to pay a fine, half of which would go to the plaintiff, and the other half to the officers of the office.

Besides these conveyances there are a great number of chariots and coaches belonging to noblemen and to gentlemen. Some are magnificent, and most are drawn by fine and excellent horses. The chariots belonging to noblemen are recognisable by the small gilt coronets placed at each of the four corners of the imperial; those belonging to dukes have ducal coronets, and so on. These fine chariots, behind which stand two or three footmen attired in rich liveries, are certainly a great ornament to a town, and a convenience to rich people, but they are a great hindrance to those who are not wealthy and go on foot, for the streets being generally very muddy, the passers-by get terribly be-spattered and dirty. Pedestrians, it is true, would be far worse off were there not on either side of the street a sort of elevated footpath for their convenience, but I think I have already told you of this.

Near the palace and in its vicinity there are more than three hundred sedan chairs for hire; like the cabs, they are found in the principal streets and thoroughfares. Chairs are very convenient and pleasant for use, the bearers going so fast that you have some difficulty in keeping up with them on foot. I do not believe that in the whole of Europe better or more dexterous bearers are to be found; all foreigners are surprised at their strength and skill. Like coaches, sedan chairs are most convenient for the wealthy, but often very embarrassing for those of another class, for these chairs are allowed to be carried on the foot-paths, and when a person does not take heed, or a stranger does not understand the 'Have care,' or 'By your leave, sir,' of the bearers, and does not make room to let them pass, he will run a great risk of being knocked down, for the bearers go very fast and cannot turn aside with their burden.

I went through this experience on first coming to London. Not understanding the 'By your leave' addressed to me, I did not draw aside, and repented quickly, for I received a tremendous push which hurled me four feet further on, and I should undoubtedly have fallen on my back had it not been for the wall of a house which broke my fall, but much to the injury of my arm. To my cost I thus learnt what the cry of the bearer means. Sedan chairs are also numbered and there is an office where you can go and make your complaint if cheated by your bearers – César de Saussure, *A Foreign View of England in the Reigns of George I and George II*, 1725-9.

Oars and Sculls

The little boats upon the Thames, which are only for carrying of persons, are light and pretty; some are rowed by one man, others by two. The former are called scullers and the latter oars. They are reckoned at several thousands, but though there are indeed a great many, I believe the number is exaggerated. The city of London being very long, it is a great conveniency to be able sometimes to make use of this way of carriage. You sit at your ease upon cushions and have a board to lean against, but generally they have no covering, unless a cloth which the watermen set up immediately, in case of need, over a few hoops, and sometimes you are wet to the skin for all this. It is easy to conceive that the oars go faster than the sculls and accordingly their pay is doubled. You never have no disputes with them, for you can go to no part either of London or the country, above or below it, but the rate is fixed by authority, everything is regulated and printed. The same is done with respect to Hackney-coaches and carts for the carriage of goods — César de Saussure, *A Foreign View of England in the Reigns of George I and George II*, 1725-9.

17 Law and Crime

An Interpretation of the Several Qualities of Rogues

Hoisters, such as help one another upon their backs in the night-time to get into windows.

Sneakers, such as sneak into a house by night or day to steal.

Sneaking Budgers, such as pilfer things off of a stall.

Tail-drawers, such as take gentlemen's swords from their sides, at the turning of a corner, or in a crowd.

Clouters, such as take handkerchiefs out of folk's pockets.

Files, such as dive into folk's pockets for money or watches.

Dubbers, such as rob dwelling-houses, warehouses, coach-houses, or stables, by picking the locks thereof.

Cheiving-layers, such as cut the leathers which bears up coaches behind, and whilst the coachmen come off their boxes to see what's the matter, they take a box or trunk from under his seat.

Wagon-layers, such as wait just out of town for wagons coming in or going out of town in a dark morning, to take boxes, or any portable bundles out of them.

Prad-layers, such as cut bags from behind horses as people ride along in the dark.

Horse-pads, such as rob in the highway on horseback.

Foot-pads, such as rob passengers.

Mill-layers, such as break into houses, by forcing doors or shutters open with betties or chisels.

Till-divers, such as go into shops with pretence to buy something, and with several excuses of seeing this thing, and that thing, to make the shopkeeper turn his back often, they put a small whalebone, daubed at the end with bird-lime, into the till of the counter, and draw up the money; but this employment is now grown something out of date.

Running-smoblers, such as go into a shop in the night, where people are busy in the back-room, or elsewhere, and, snatching something that's nearest them, they run away with it.

Fam-layers, such as go into goldsmith's shops, with pretence to buy a

120

ring, and several being laid upon the counter, they palm one or two by means of a little ale held in a spoon over the fire, with which the palm, being daubed, any light thing sticks to it.

Faggot and Stall, such as break into people's houses, and, taking away what they please, gag all therein.

Impudent Stealers, such as cut out the backs of coaches, and take things out of them.

Sweetners, such as drop money before people, and, taking out of sight, inveigle a man (after a hot dispute with some of their accomplices, who earnestly claim halves of what they find) into a tavern they use, where they draw him into cards, dice, or buckle and thong, which they planted in some visible place, and win all his money: these sort of vermin likewise go about the country to cheat people of their money, by the legerdemain slight of cups and ball, and luck in a bag; this is a function too that has not flourished since the late Act for Vagabonds.

Night-gamester, such as rob parks at nights for venison, which proves to be dear if they are taken.

But of all these, house-breaker, under three denominations, viz. hoister, dubber and mill-layer, is the most famous and heroic employment of them all, and in one time exceeds that of the highway.

Some are ingenious at the lob, which is going into a shop to have a guinea or a pistole changed, and the change being given the bringer palms two or three shillings, and then says there wants so much, which the shop-keeper, telling over again, says it is true, and very innocently makes up the sum.

As for the female proficients, they consist chiefly in these:

Shop-lifting, which almost everybody understands.

Buttock and Twang, which is walking to be picked up, and, frightening him that does it with her pretended husband, after she has picked his pocket, so that the fool runs gladly away without his watch or money.

Buttock and File, which is the same with the other; only this is the better-natured beast of the two, and performs her stage before she takes her wages, which may be some satisfaction to the ass she carries.

From *Memoirs of the Right Villainous John Hall*, 1708.

Take a Warning

Here the author tells of dangers to be avoided, notably thieves, in London streets.

> Where the mob gathers, swiftly shoot along,
> Nor idly mingle in the noisy throng.
> Lured by the silver hilt, amid the swarm,
> The subtle artist will thy side disarm.
> Nor is thy flaxen wig with safety worn;
> High on the shoulder, in the basket born,
> Lurks the sly boy; whose hand to rapine bred,
> Plucks off the curling honours of the head.
> Here dives the skulking thief, with practised slight,
> And unfelt fingers make thy pocket light.
> Where's now thy watch, with all its trinkets flown?
> And thy late snuff-box is no more thy own.

John Gay, *Trivia, or The Art of Walking the Streets of London*, 1716.

The General Complaint

Now it is the general complaint of the taverns, the coffee-houses, the shopkeepers and others, that their customers are afraid when it is dark to come to their houses and shops for fear that their hats and wigs should be snitched from their heads or their swords taken from their sides, or that they may be blinded, knocked down, cut or stabbed; nay, the coaches cannot secure them, but they are likewise cut and robbed in the public streets, &c. By which means the traffic of the City is much interrupted − City Marshal, Hitchin, *A true Discovery of the Conduct of Receivers and Thief Takers in and about the City of London*, 1718.

Singular Case of Catherine Jones Tried for Bigamy and Acquitted, 5 September 1719

Catherine Jones was indicted at the Old Bailey, on the 5th of September, 1719, for marrying Constantine Boone during the life of her former husband, John Rowland.

Proof was made that she was married to Rowland, in the year 1713, at a house in the Mint, Southwark, and that six years afterwards, while her husband was abroad, she was again married, in the same house, to Constantine Boone; but Rowland, soon returning to England, caused his wife to be indicted for this crime.

The prisoner did not hesitate to acknowledge the double marriage, but insisted that the latter was illegal, as Boone was an hermaphrodite, and had been shewn as such at Southwark and Bartholomew fairs, and at other places.

To prove this a person swore that he knew Boone when a child, that his (or *her*) mother dressed *it* in girls apparel, and caused it to be instructed in needle-work, till it had attained the age of twelve years, when it *turned man, and went to sea.*

These last words were those of the deposition; and the fact was confirmed by Boone, who appeared in court, acknowledged being an hermaphrodite, and having been publickly shewn in that character.

Other witnesses deposed that the female sex prevailed over that of the male in the party in question; on which the jury acquitted the prisoner.

It is impossible to describe how much this affair was the subject of the public conversation at, and long after, the time that it happened: and it would be idle to make any serious remarks on it. We can only express our astonishment that an hermaphrodite should think of such a glaring absurdity as the taking a wife! — from *The Newgate Calendar, c.* 1774.

Articles of Information Produced against Jonathan Wild in Court

He became head of a large corporation of criminals, and opened offices in London for the recovery and restoration of property stolen by his accomplices. He betrayed such thieves as would not share with him, till for theft and receiving he was tried and hanged at Tyburn, 25 May 1725.

In 1725 Defoe wrote about him in Life and Actions; *and Fielding in 1743 produced a satirical romance,* Jonathan Wild the Great.

I. That for many years past he had been a confederate with great numbers of highwaymen, pick-pockets, housebreakers, shop-lifters, and other thieves.

II. That he had formed a kind of corporation of thieves, of which he was the head or director, and that notwithstanding his pretended services, in detecting and prosecuting offenders, he procured such only to be hanged as concealed their booty, or refused to share it with him.

III. That he had divided the town and country into so many districts, and appointed distinct gangs for each, who regularly accounted with him for their robberies. That he had also a particular set to steal at churches in time of divine service: and likewise other moving detachments to attend at court, on birth-days, balls, &c. and at both houses of parliament, circuits, and country fairs.

IV. That the persons employed by him were for the most part felons convict, who had returned from transportation before the time, for which they were transported, was expired; and that he made choice of them to be his agents, because they could not be legal evidences against him, and because he had it in his power to take from them what part of the stolen goods he thought fit, and otherwise use them ill, or hang them as he pleased.

V. That he had from time to time supplied such convicted felons with money and cloaths, and lodged them in his own house, the better to conceal them: particularly some, against whom there are now informations for counterfeiting and diminishing broad pieces and guineas.

VI. That he had not only been a receiver of stolen goods, as well as of writings of all kinds, for near fifteen years past, but had frequently been a confederate, and robbed along with the above-mentioned convicted felons.

VII. That, in order to carry on these vile practices, to gain some credit with the ignorant multitude, he usually carried a short silver staff, as a badge of authority from the government, which he used to produce, when he himself was concerned in robbing.

VIII. That he had, under his care and direction, several warehouses for receiving and concealing stolen goods; and also a ship for carrying off jewels, watches, and other valuable goods, to Holland, where he had a superannuated thief for his factor.

IX. That he kept in pay several artists to make alterations, and transform watches, seals, snuff-boxes, rings, and other valuable things, that they might not be known, several of which he used to present to such persons as he thought might be of service to him.

X. That he seldom or never helped the owners to the notes and papers they had lost, unless he found them able exactly to specify and describe them, and then often insisted on more than half the value.

XI. And lastly, it appears that he has often sold human blood, by procuring false evidence to swear persons into facts they were not guilty of; sometimes to prevent them from being evidences against himself, and at other times for the sake of the great reward given by the government – from *The Newgate Calendar, c.* 1774.

At the Old Bailey

The same day, at noon, the Sessions ended at the Old Bailey, when the 2 following persons received sentence of death, viz. John Turner, for breaking into the apartments of Mrs Turner, who was an intimate of his father's, near Queenhithe, and stealing from thence 1 guinea, £5 1s. in silver, and several wearing apparel; and Anne Palmer, alias Hinks, for stealing £81s. in money, and goods to the value of 38s., the property of Mr. Sam. Ruffel. . . . Five were burnt in the hand, and 30 were cast for transportation. . . . Seven were burnt in the hand, and about 20 ordered for transportation. . . . Eight were burnt in the hand – *The Grub Street Journal*, 21 October 1731.

A Successful Tea Smuggler

Smuggling, to run goods ashore, or bring them in by stealth without paying the customs was very common in the eighteenth century.

Since an excise duty of 4s. per pound was laid on tea, it has brought an average of £130,000 a year into the exchequer, which is but for 650,000 pounds weight of tea. But that the real consumption is vastly greater a single fact will prove. Some years ago the Treasurer of our East India Company received a letter from Holland intimating that one person in the Province of Zeeland smuggled yearly for England no less than half a million pounds. Though this seemed incredible, the directors, upon inquiry, were convinced of the fact that such a person there was who, some years before had been but an English sailor, was now married to a woman that kept a china shop. He had so well managed affairs that he had four sloops of his own constantly employed in smuggling; that the quantity of tea which he was supposed to export had not at all been magnified, and that he had more guineas and English coin in his house than any banker in England – *A Proposal for Preventing of Running Goods.*

An Account of Richard Turpin

Dick Turpin was a notorious highway robber, whose fictitious exploits on his mare 'Black Bess' became legendary. Son of an Essex innkeeper, he began his career by cattle-stealing when a butcher's apprentice. In reality he was without scruples or mercy, and was a smuggler and housebreaker, as well as a highwayman. The account below tells how he was caught and hanged on 10 April 1739.

For a considerable time did Turpin skulk about the forest, having been deprived of his retreat in the cave since he shot the servant of Mr Thompson. On the examination of this cave there were found two shirts, two pairs of stockings, a piece of ham, and part of a bottle of wine.

Some vain attempts were made to take this notorious offender into custody; and among the rest the huntsman of a gentleman in the neighbourhood went in search of him with bloodhounds. Turpin perceiving them, got into a tree, under which the hounds passed, to his inexpressible terror, so that he determined to make a retreat into Yorkshire.

Going first to Long-Sutton in Lincolnshire, he stole some horses; for which he was taken into custody; but he escaped from the constable as he was conducting him before a magistrate, and hastened to Welton in Yorkshire, where he went by the name of John Palmer, and assumed the character of a gentleman.

He now frequently went into Lincolnshire, where he stole horses, which he brought into Yorkshire, and either sold or exchanged them.

He often accompanied the neighbouring gentlemen on their parties of hunting and shooting; and one evening, on a return from an expedition of the latter kind, he wantonly shot a cock belonging to his landlord. On this Mr Hall, a neighbour, said, 'You have done wrong in shooting your landlord's cock;' to which Turpin replied, that if he would stay while he loaded his gun he would shoot him also.

Irritated by this insult, Mr Hall informed the landlord of what had passed; and application being made to some magistrates, a warrant was granted for the apprehension of the offender, who being taken into custody, and carried before a bench of justices then assembled at the quarter sessions at Beverley, they demanded security for his good behaviour, which he being unable or unwilling to give, was committed to Bridewell.

On enquiry it appeared that he made frequent journies into Lincolnshire, and on his return he always abounded in money, and was likewise in possession of several horses; so that it was conjectured that he was a horse-stealer and highwayman.

On this the magistrates went to him on the following day, and demanded who he was, where he had lived, and what was his employment. He replied in substance, 'that about two years ago he had lived at Long-Sutton in Lincolnshire, and was by trade a butcher; but that having contracted several debts for sheep that proved rotten, he was obliged to abscond, and come to live in Yorkshire.'

The magistrates not being satisfied with this tale, commissioned the clerk of the peace to write into Lincolnshire, to make the necessary enquiries respecting the supposed John Palmer. The letter was carried by a special messenger, who brought an answer from a magistrate in the neighbourhood, importing that John Palmer was well known, though he had never carried on trade there: that he had been accused of sheep-stealing, for which he had been in custody, but had made his escape from the peace-officers; and that there were several informations lodged against him for horse-stealing.

Hereupon the magistrates thought it prudent to remove him to York Castle, where he had not been more than a month, when two persons from Lincolnshire came and claimed a mare and foal, and likewise a horse, which he had stolen in that country.

After he had been about four months in prison he wrote the following letter to his brother in Essex.

'Dear Brother,   York, Feb. 6, 1739

'I Am sorry to acquaint you that I am now under confinement in York Castle, for horse-stealing. If I could procure an evidence from London to give me a character, that would go a great way towards my being acquitted. I had not been long in this country before my being apprehended, so that it would pass off the readier. For Heaven's sake, dear brother, do not neglect me; you will know what I mean, when I say—

'I am Yours,
'John Palmer'

This letter being returned, unopened, to the Post-Office in Essex, because the brother would not pay the postage of it, was accidentally seen by Mr Smith, a schoolmaster, who having taught Turpin to write, immediately knew his hand, on which he carried the letter to a magistrate, who broke it open; by which it was discovered that the supposed John Palmer was the real Richard Turpin.

Hereupon the magistrates of Essex dispatched Mr Smith to York, who immediately selected him from all the other prisoners in the castle. This Mr Smith and another gentleman afterwards proved his identity on his trial.

On the rumour that the noted Turpin was a prisoner in York Castle, persons flocked from all parts of the country to take a view of him, and debates ran very high whether he was the real person or not. Among others who visited him was a young fellow who pretended to know the famous Turpin, and having regarded him a considerable time with looks of great attention, he told the keeper he would bet him half a guinea that he was not Turpin; on which the prisoner, whispering the keeper, said 'Lay him the wager, and I'll go your halves.'

When this notorious malefactor was brought to trial he was convicted on two indictments, and received sentence of death.

After conviction he wrote to his father, imploring him to intercede with a gentleman and lady of rank, to make interest that his sentence might be remitted; and that he might be transported. The father did what was in his power; but the notoriety of his character was such, that no persons would exert themselves in his favour.

This man lived in the most gay and thoughtless manner after conviction, regardless of all considerations of futurity, and affecting to make a jest of the dreadful fate that awaited him.

Not many days before his execution he purchased a new fustian frock and a pair of pumps, in order to wear them at the time of his death; and, on the day before, he hired five poor men, at ten shillings each, to follow the cart as mourners; and he gave hatbands and gloves to several other persons; and he also left a ring, and some other articles, to a married woman in Lincolnshire, with whom he had been acquainted.

On the morning of his death he was put into a cart, and being followed by his mourners, as above-mentioned, he was drawn to the place of execution, in his way to which he bowed to the spectators with an air of the most astonishing indifference and intrepidity.

When he came to the fatal tree, he ascended the ladder; when his right leg trembling, he stamped it down with an air of assumed courage, as if he was ashamed to be observed to discover any signs of fear. Having conversed with the executioner about half an hour, he threw himself off the ladder and expired in a few minutes.

He suffered at York, on the tenth of April, 1739.

The spectators of the execution seemed to be much affected at the fate of this man, who was distinguished by the comeliness of his appearance. The corpse was brought to the Blue Boar, in Castle-Gate,

York, where it remained till the next morning, when it was interred in the Church-yard of St George's parish, with an inscription on the coffin, with the initials of his name, and his age — from *The Newgate Calendar, c.* 1774.

Treatment of Informers, and the Results

The perjuries of informers were ... so flagrant and common, that the people thought all informations malicious, or at least, thinking themselves oppressed by the law, they looked upon every man that promoted its execution as their enemy, and therefore now began to declare war against informers, many of whom they treated with great cruelty and some they murdered in the streets. By their obstinacy they at last wearied the magistrates, and by their violence they intimidated those who might be inclined to make discoveries, so that the law ... has been now [1743] for some years totally disused, nor has any man been found willing to engage in a task at once odious as endless, or to punish offences which every day multiplied, and on which the whole body of the common people, a body very formidable when united, was universally engaged — Samuel Johnson, *Gentleman's Magazine*, 1743.

The Execution of Lord Kilmarnock, 1745

Horace Walpole reports on the occasion. Thousands, including the 'quality', turned out for the spectacle.

He took no notice of the crowd, only to desire that the baize might be lifted up from the rails, that the mob might see the spectacle ... He then took off his bag, coat and waistcoat, with great composure, and after some trouble put on a napkin-cap, and then several times tried the block; the executioner, who was in white, with a white apron, out of tenderness concealing the axe behind himself. At last the Earl knelt down, with a visible unwillingness to depart, and after five minutes dropped his handkerchief, the signal, and his head was cut off at once, only hanging by a bit of skin, and was received in a scarlet cloth by four of the undertaker's men kneeling, who wrapped it up and put it into the coffin with the body; orders having been given not to expose the heads, as used to be the custom.

Poverty and Crime

Though most of the rogues who infest the public roads and streets, indeed almost all the thieves in general, are vagabonds in the true sense of the word, being wanderers from their lawful place of abode, very few of them will be proved vagabonds within the words of the act of parliament. These vagabonds do, indeed, get their livelihood by thieving, and not as petty beggars or petty chapmen [pedlars]; and have their lodging not in alehouses, etc., but in private houses, where many of them resort together, and unite in gangs, paying each 2d per night for their beds.

The following account I have had from Mr. Welch, the high-constable of Holborn; and none who know that gentleman, will want any confirmation of the truth of it. 'That in the parish of St. Giles's there are great numbers of houses set apart for the reception of idle persons and vagabonds, who have their lodging there for twopence a night; that in the above parish, and in St. George, Bloomsbury, one woman alone occupies seven of these houses, all properly accommodated with miserable beds from the cellar to the garret, for such twopenny lodgers, the price of a double bed being no more than threepence; these places are no less provided for drunkenness, gin being sold in them all at a penny a quartern, so that the smallest sum of money serves for intoxication; that in the execution of search-warrants Mr. Welch rarely finds less than twenty of these houses open for the receipt of all comers at the latest hours; that in one of these houses, and that not a large one, he hath numbered fifty-eight persons of both sexes, the stench of whom was so intolerable that it compelled him in a short time to quit the place.' Nay, I can add, what I myself once saw in the parish of Shoreditch, where two little houses were emptied of near seventy men and women.

If one considers the destruction of all morality, decency, and modesty: the swearing, and drunkenness which is eternally carrying on in these houses, on the one hand, and the excessive poverty and misery of most of the inhabitants on the other, it seems doubtful whether they are more the objects of detestation or compassion; for such is the poverty of these wretches, that upon searching all the above number, the money found upon all of them did not amount to one shilling; and I have been credibly informed that a single loaf hath supplied a whole family with their provisions for a week. Lastly, if any of these miserable creatures fall sick (and it is almost a miracle that stench, vermin, and want, should ever suffer them to be well) they are turned out in the streets by their merciless host or hostess, where, unless some parish officer of extraordinary charity relieves them, they are sure miserably to perish, with the addition of hunger and cold to their disease.

This picture, which is taken from the life, will appear strange to many; for the evil here described is, I am confident, very little known, especially to those of the better sort. Indeed this is the only excuse, and I believe the only reason, that it hath been so long tolerated; for when we consider the number of these wretches, which, in the outskirts of the town, amounts to a great many thousands, it is a nuisance which will appear to be big with every moral and political mischief. Of these the excessive misery of the wretches themselves, oppressed with want, and sunk in every species of debauchery, and the loss of so many lives to the public, are obvious and immediate consequences.

Among other mischiefs attending this wretched nuisance, the great increase of thieves must necessarily be one. The wonder in fact is that we have not a thousand more robbers than we have; indeed, that all these wretches are not thieves must give us either a very high idea of their honesty, or a very mean one of their capacity and courage – Henry Fielding, *An Enquiry into the Causes of the late Increase of Robbers*, 1750.

The Trial of Miss Mary Blandy for Murder, 1752

Miss Mary Blandy was infatuated by Captain Cranstoun, whose wife in Scotland by letter gave up all claim to him, though the marriage was later confirmed. Soon after this Mrs Blandy died. Mr Blandy had shown strong dislike of the Captain. Cranstoun from Scotland sent Mary some powder described as 'Powders to clean Scotch pebbles.' The powder was to be given to Mr Blandy 'to conciliate him.' In fact it was poison, which Mary put into water-gruel for her father, made by Susan Gunnel, a maidservant. After an illness he died. Mary ran away from home, was caught and tried for murder.

'Upon the report of my making my escape, the gentleman who was high sheriff last year (not the present) came and told me, by order of the higher powers, he must put an iron on me. I submitted as I always do to the higher powers. Some time after he came again, and said, he must put an heavier upon me, which I have worn, my lords, till I came hither. I asked the sheriff why I was so ironed? He said, he did it by the command of some noble peer, on his hearing that I intended making my escape. I told them I never had any such thought, and I would bear it with the other cruel usage I had received on my character. The Reverend Mr Swinton, the worthy clergyman who attended me in prison, can testify I was regular at the chapel whenever I was well; sometimes I really was not able to come out, and then he attended me in my room. They have likewise published papers and depositions, which ought not to have been published, in order to represent me as the most abandoned of my sex, and to prejudice the world against me. I submit myself to your lordships, and to the worthy jury – I do assure your lordship, as I am to answer it at the great tribunal, where I must appear, I am as innocent as the child unborn of the death of my father. I would not endeavour to save my life at the expense of truth. I really thought the powder an innocent, inoffensive thing, and I gave it to procure his love (meaning towards Cranstoun.) – It has been mentioned, I should say I was ruined. My lord, when a young woman loses her character, is not that her ruin? Why then should this expression be construed in so wide a sense? Is not ruining my character to have such a thing laid to my charge? And, whatever may be the event of his trial, I am ruined most effectually.'

The trial lasted eleven hours, and then the judge summed up the evidence, mentioning the scandalous behaviour of some people respecting the prisoner in printing and publishing what they called depositions taken before the coroner, relating to the affair before them: to which he added, 'I hope you have not seen them; but if you have, I must tell you, as you are men of sense and probity, that you must divest yourselves of every prejudice that can arise from thence, and attend merely to the evidence that has now been given.'

The judge then summed up the evidence with the utmost candour; and the jury, having considered the affair, found her guilty without going out of court.

After conviction, she behaved with the utmost decency and resignation. She was attended by the Reverend Mr Swinton, from whose hands she received the sacrament on the day before her execution, declaring that she did not know there was any thing hurtful in the powders she had given her father.

The night before her death she spent in devotion; and at nine in the morning she left her apartment, being dressed in a black bombazine, and having her arms bound with black ribbons.

The clergyman attended her to the place of execution, to which she walked with the utmost solemnity of deportment; and, when there, acknowledged her fault in administering the powders to her father, but declared that, as she must soon appear before the most awful tribunal, she had no idea of doing injury, nor any suspicions that the powders were of a poisonous nature.

Having ascended some steps of the ladder, she said, 'Gentlemen, don't hang me high, for the sake of decency.' Being desired to go something higher, she turned about, and expressed her apprehensions that she should fall. The rope being put round her neck, she pulled her handkerchief over her face, and was turned-off, on holding out a book of devotions which she had been reading.

The crowd of spectators assembled on this occasion was immense; and, when she had hung the usual time, she was cut down, and the body, being put into a hearse, was conveyed to Henley, and interred with her parents, at one o'clock on the following morning.

She was executed at Oxford, on the 6th of April, 1752 – from *The Newgate Calendar, c.* 1774.

18 News

Coffee-Houses and the Latest News

In London there are a great number of coffee-houses, most of which, to tell the truth, are not over clean or well furnished, owing to the quantity of people who resort to these places and because of the smoke, which would quickly destroy good furniture. Englishmen are great drinkers. In these coffee-houses you can partake of chocolate, tea, or coffee, and of all sorts of liquors, served hot; also in many places you can have wine, punch, or ale. . . . What attracts enormously in these coffee-houses are the gazettes and other public papers. All Englishmen are great newsmongers. Workmen habitually begin the day by going to coffee-rooms in order to read the latest news. I have often seen shoeblacks and other persons of that class club together to purchase a farthing paper. . . . Some coffee-houses are a resort for learned scholars and for wits; others are the resort of dandies or of politicians, or again of professional newsmongers – César de Saussure, *A Foreign View of England in the Reigns of George I and George II,* 1725-9.

The Importance of Advertisements

And whereas by reason of the great Number of News-Papers daily Printed, and that few Persons Advertise in more than some one of them, and that none except the most eminent Coffee-Houses take in all the Daily Printed Papers, and that few Gentlemen or Others who frequent those Houses, read every Paper there taken in, the Advertisement remains unknown to great Numbers of Persons, to the Prejudice and Inconvenience of the Advertiser. It is apprehended that the Publication made by this Paper will be very general and useful, all the Advertisements being collected together, every Person may readily find out whatever can properly fall under the Denomination of an

Advertisement, without having recourse to any other Paper — *The Daily Advertiser.*

'The Champion' Acts to Prevent Piracies

If *News-Papers*, are only calculated to *kill Time*, the present Set will answer that End very effectually. But, if to *inform*, or even to *entertain* is the Tenure of their Charter, a *new One* is absolutely necessary to save it from being forfeited beyond Redemption.

On this Presumption, this Paper was, a few Months ago, set up; which had, at least, something of Novelty, if no more, to recommend it. But, having a vigorous *Opposition* on all Hands to struggle with (*Booksellers*, who were Sharers in the Profit of other News-Papers; *Coffeemen*, who thought they were encumbered with too many already; *Place-men*, because it made War on their Patron; *Patriot-writers*, because it might possibly interfere with their own; and *Hawkers* in Fee with them all) it made its Way but slowly, nay was actually given out for *Dead*, long ago.

And no sooner was it received with Approbation by some, and Indulgence by all unprejudiced Readers, but the *Craftsman*, *London Evening Post*, &c. and many of the *Country Papers* began to enrich themselves with its Spoils; which (tho' their Sanction may be no Proof of its Merit) argued, at least, that it was not *unacceptable* to the Publick.

Rather, therefore, than give Way to such *Piracies* any longer, it has been thought expedient to alter the *Time* of publishing this Paper, called the *Champion*, from *Tuesday, Thursday* and *Saturday* Mornings, to the *Evening* of the same Days, when it will be punctually sent to such publick or private Houses, as shall order it in, by

J. GRAHAM, under the *Inner Temple-Gate*, opposite *Chancery Lane*, in *Fleet Street*, where Advertisements and Letters for the Author are taken in.

It will contain, as before,

I An Essay on the *Manners* or *Politicks* of the Times.

II Frequently, new Articles of Intelligence.

III The News of Two Days, Foreign and Domestick, stated and digested in a peculiar Manner.

IV Extracts from, or Remarks upon such Books, Poems, Pamphlets, &c. as are worthy the Notice of the Publick.

  * In the Craftsman *of last* Saturday, *no less than ten Paragraphs*

were taken verbatim *from the* Champion; *besides the* remarkable *one* in Mourning — *The Champion*, 10 April 1740.

Soul of an Advertisement

Advertisements are now so numerous that they are very negligently perused, and it is therefore become necessary to gain attention by magnificence of promises, and by eloquence sublime and sometimes pathetic. Promise, large promise is the soul of an Advertisement — Dr Johnson, *Idler*, 1759.

19 Famous People

John Churchill, Duke of Marlborough (1650–1722)

It has been said that as a military strategist and a tactician, as a war statesman and war diplomatist, Marlborough stands second to no Englishman in history. G.M. Trevelyan adds further praise, 'Marlborough protected the advent of the much needed age of reason, toleration and common sense.'

He is a man of birth: about the middle height, and the best figure in the world: his features without fault, fine sparkling eyes, good teeth, and his complexion such a mixture of white and red that the fairer sex might envy: in brief, except for his legs, which are too thin, one of the handsomest men ever seen. . . . He expresses himself well, and even his very bad French is agreeable; his voice is harmonious, and as a speaker in his own language he is reckoned among the best. His address is most courteous, and while his handsome and well-graced countenance engages everyone in his favour at first sight, his perfect manners and his gentleness win over even those who start with a prejudice or grudge against him – Sicco van Goslinga, *Memoires*, quoted by Sir Winston Churchill in *Marlborough*.

Sarah Jennings, Duchess of Marlborough, 1660-1744, by Sir Godfrey Kneller. This portrait is now at Althorp in Northamptonshire, the home of the Earl Spencer. She was a beautiful termagant, and married John Churchill, later 1st Duke of Marlborough. She became groom of the stole, mistress of the robes, keeper of the privy purse, and bosom friend of Queen Anne.

137

Doctor Richard Bentley (1662—1742)

English classical scholar and critic. His Dissertation upon the Epistles of Phalaris *established his reputation throughout Europe.*

As for the *hat*, I must acknowledge it was of formidable dimensions, yet I was accustomed to treat it with great familiarity, and if it had ever been further from the hand of its owner than the peg upon the back of his great armchair, I might have been dispatched to fetch it, for he was disabled by the palsy in his latter days; but the hat never strayed from its place. . . .

I have broken in upon him many times in his hours of study, when he would put his book aside, ring his hand-bell for his servant, and be led to his shelves to take down a picture-book for my amusement. I do not say his good-nature always gained its object, as the pictures which his books generally supplied me with were anatomical drawings of dissected bodies, very little calculated to communicate delight; but he had nothing better to produce; and surely such an effort on his part, however unsuccessful, was no feature of a cynic; a cynic *should be made of sterner stuff*. . . .

His ordinary style of conversation was naturally lofty, and his frequent use of *thou* and *thee* with his familiars carried with it a kind of dictatorial tone, that savoured more of the closet than the court; this is readily admitted, and this on first approaches might mislead a stranger; but the native candour and inherent tenderness of his heart could not long be veiled from observation, for his feelings and affections were at once too impulsive to be long repressed, and he too careless of concealment to attempt at qualifying them — Richard Cumberland (his grandson), *Memoirs of Richard Cumberland.*

Jonathan Swift (1667—1745)

English clergyman, Tory pamphleteer, masterly satirist; Dean of St Patrick's, Dublin. Gulliver's Travels *is his world-famous satire.*

He was in the decline of life when I knew him. His friendship was an honour to me, and to say the truth, I have even drawn down advantage from his errors. I have beheld him in all humours and dispositions, and

I have formed various speculations from the several weaknesses, to which I observed him liable. His capacity and strength of mind were undoubtedly equal to any task whatever. His pride, his spirit, or his ambition, call it by what name you please, was boundless: but, his views were checked in his younger years, and the anxiety of that disappointment had a visible effect upon all his actions. He was sour and severe, but not absolutely ill-natured. He was sociable only to particular friends, and to them only at particular hours. He knew politeness more than he practised it. He was a mixture of avarice, and generosity: the former was frequently prevalent, the latter, seldom appeared, unless excited by compassion. He was open to adulation, and could not, or would not, distinguish between low flattery, and just applause. His abilities rendered him superior to envy. He was undisguised and perfectly sincere. I am induced to think, that he entered into orders, more from some private and fixed resolution, than from absolute choice: be that as it may, he performed the duties of the church with great punctuality, and a decent degree of devotion. He read prayers rather in a strong nervous voice, than in a graceful manner: and altho' he has been often accused of irreligion, nothing of that kind appeared in his conversation or behaviour. His cast of mind induced him to think, and speak more of politics than of religion. His perpetual views were directed towards power, and his chief aim was to be removed into *England*: but when he found himself entirely disappointed, he turned his thoughts to opposition, and became the patron of *Ireland*, in which country he was born – the Earl of Orrery, *Remarks on the Life and Writings of Dr Jonathan Swift*, 1751.

Sir Robert Walpole, First Earl of Orford (1676–1745)

English statesman, leader of Whig administration, in effect first British Prime Minister, 1721–42. Established responsibility of Cabinet and Prime Minister to Parliament.

In private life he was good-natured, cheerful, social; inelegant in his manners, loose in his morals, he had a coarse, strong wit, which he was too free of for a man in his station, as it is always inconsistent with dignity. He was very able as a Minister, but without a certain elevation of mind, necessary for great good, or great mischief. Profuse and appetent, his ambition was subservient to his design of making a great fortune – He had more of the Mazarin than of the Richelieu – He would do mean things for profit, and never thought of doing great ones for glory. He was both the best parliament-man, and the ablest manager of parliament, that I believe ever lived. An artful rather than eloquent speaker, he saw, as by intuition, the disposition of the house, and pressed or receded accordingly. So clear in stating the most intricate matters, especially in the finances, that, whilst he was speaking the most ignorant thought that they understood what they really did not. Money, not prerogative, was the chief engine of his administration; and he employed it with a success, which in a manner disgraced humanity. He was not, it is true, the inventor of that shameful method of governing which had been gaining ground insensibly ever since Charles the Second, but with uncommon skill and unbounded profusion he brought it to that perfection, which at this time dishonours and distresses this country, and which (if not checked, and God knows how it can be now checked) must ruin it.

Besides this powerful engine of government, he had a most extra-ordinary talent of persuading and working men up to his purpose — A hearty kind of frankness, which sometimes seemed impudence, made people think that he led them into his secrets, whilst the impoliteness of his manners seemed to attest his sincerity. When he found anybody proof against pecuniary temptations, which alas! was but seldom, he had recourse to a still worse art: for he laughed at and ridiculed all notions of public virtue, and the love of one's country, calling them *The chimerical school-boy flights of classical learning*; declaring himself at the same time, *No Saint, no Spartan, no Reformer* – Lord Chesterfield, *Characters of Eminent Personages of His Own Time*, 1777.

Bolingbroke, Henry St John, First Viscount (1678–1751)

Supporter of Harley and the Tory party; founded The Brothers' Club, 1711. Advocated type of democratic Toryism anticipating that of Disraeli.

As to Lord Bolingbroke's general character, it was so mixed that he had certainly some qualifications that the greatest men might be proud of, and many which the worst would be ashamed of. He had fine talents, a natural eloquence, great quickness, a happy memory, and very extensive knowledge: but he was vain much beyond the general run of mankind, timid, false, injudicious, and ungrateful; elate and insolent in power, dejected and servile in disgrace. Few people ever believed him without being deceived, or trusted him without being betrayed. He was one to whom prosperity was no advantage, and adversity no instruction. He had brought his affairs to that pass that he was almost as much distressed in his private fortune as desperate in his political views, and was upon such a foot in the world that no king would employ him, no party support him, and few particulars defend him. His enmity was the contempt of those he attacked, and his friendship a weight and reproach to those he adhered to. Those who were most partial to him could not but allow that he was ambitious without fortitude, and enterprising without resolution; that he was fawning without insinuation, and insincere without art; that he had admirers without friendship, and followers without attachment; parts without probity, knowledge without conduct, and experience without judgment. This was certainly his character and situation; but since it is the opinion of the wise, the speculative, and the learned, that most men are born with the same propensities, actuated by the same passions, and conducted by the same original principles, and differing only in the manner of pursuing the same ends, I shall not so far chime in with the bulk of Lord Bolingbroke's contemporaries as to pronounce he had more failings than any man ever had; but it is impossible to see all that is written, and hear all that is said of him, and not allow that if he had not a worse heart than the rest of mankind, at least he must have had much worse luck — Lord Hervey, *Memoirs.*

Alexander Pope (1688–1744)

English classical poet and critic. Works include mock-heroic epic The Rape of the Lock, *1714, satirical* Dunciad, *and* An Essay on Man *vindicating deism.*

The person of Pope is well-known not to have been formed by the nicest model ... and is described as protuberant before and behind. He is said to have been beautiful in his infancy; but he was of a constitution originally feeble and weak; and as bodies of a tender frame are easily distorted, his deformity was probably in part the effect of his application. His stature was so low that, to bring him to a level with common tables, it was necessary to raise his seat. But his face was not displeasing, and his eyes were animated and vivid.

Most of what can be told ... was communicated by a female domestic of the Earl of Oxford, who knew him perhaps after the middle of life. He was then so weak as to stand in perpetual need of female attendance; extremely sensible of cold, so that he wore a kind of fur doublet, under a shirt of very coarse warm linen with fine sleeves. When he rose, he was invested in bodice made by stiff canvas, being scarce able to hold himself erect till they were laced, and he then put on a flannel waistcoat. One side was contracted. His legs were so slender that he enlarged their bulk with three pairs of stockings, which were drawn on and off by the maid; for he was not able to dress or undress himself, and neither went to bed nor rose without help. His weakness made it very difficult for him to be clean.

His hair had fallen almost all away; and he used to dine sometimes with Lord Oxford, privately, in a velvet cap. His dress of ceremony was black, with a tye-wig, and a little sword — Samuel Johnson, *Lives of the Poets.*

James Francis Edward Stuart, the Old Pretender (1688–1766)

Son of James II. Claim to English throne frustrated by Act of Settlement, 1701, excluding male Stuart line.

The Chevalier de St. George is tall, meagre, melancholy in his aspect. Enthusiasm and disappointment have stamped a solemnity on his person which rather creates pity than respect.... Without the particular features of any Stuart, the Chevalier has the strong lines and fatality of air peculiar to them all. From the first moment I saw him, I never doubted the legitimacy of his birth — Horace Walpole, *Memoirs.*

His person was tall and thin, seeming to be lean rather than to fill as he grows in years. His countenance was pale, yet he seems to be sanguine in his constitution, and has something of a vivacity in his eye that perhaps would have been more visible, if he had not been under dejected circumstances and surrounded with discouragements, which it must be acknowledged, were sufficient to alter the complexion even of his soul as well as of his body. His speech was grave, and not very clearly expressing his thoughts, nor overmuch to the purpose, but his words were few, and his behaviour and temper seemed always composed.... Neither can I say I ever saw him smile..... We saw nothing in him that looked like spirit. He never appeared with cheerfulness and vigour to animate us. Our men began to despise him; some asked if he could speak. His countenance looked extremely heavy – *True Account of the Proceedings at Perth*, by a Rebel.

Lady Mary Wortley Montagu (1689–1762)

English writer and society leader. On return to Britain from Turkey introduced smallpox inoculation. Described Eastern life in entertaining letters.

I found her in a little miserable bedchamber of a ready-furnished house, with two tallow candles, and a bureau covered with pots and pans. On her head . . . she had an old black-laced hood, wrapped entirely round, so as to conceal all hair, or want of hair. No handkerchief, but up to her chin a kind of horseman's riding-coat . . . made of dark-green brocade, with coloured and silver flowers, and lined with furs; bodice laced, a foul dimity petticoat, sprig'd, velvet muffeteens of her arms, grey stockings, and slippers. Her face less changed in twenty years than I could have imagined. I told her so, and she was not so tolerable twenty years ago that she need have taken it for flattery – Horace Walpole, from John Timbs, *A Century of Anecdote, 1760–1860*.

Roubiliac's terra-cotta model for a bust of William Hogarth, 1697-1764. English painter, engraver. Produced series of satirical engravings, *The Harlot's Progress, The Rake's Progress, Marriage-à-la-Mode, Industry and Idleness*. He wrote *The Analysis of Beauty*.

143

John Wesley (1703–1791)

English theologian, evangelist, and founder of Methodism. During an unparalleled apostolate he travelled 250,000 miles, and preached 40,000 sermons.

The figure of Mr Wesley was remarkable. His stature was of the lowest: his habit of body in every period of life, the reverse of corpulent, and expressive of strict temperance, and continual exercise and notwithstanding his small size, his step was firm, and his appearance, till within a few years of his death, vigorous and muscular. His face, for an old man, was one of the finest we have seen. A clear, smooth forehead, an aquiline nose, an eye the brightest and most piercing that can be conceived, and a freshness of complexion, scarcely ever to be found at his years, and impressive of the most perfect health, conspired to render him a venerable and interesting figure. Few have seen him, without being struck with his appearance: and many, who have been greatly prejudiced against him, have been known to change their opinions, the moment they were introduced into his presence. In his countenance, and demeanour, there was a cheerfulness mingled with gravity; a sprightliness which was the natural result of an unusual flow of spirits, and was yet accompanied with every mark of the most serene tranquillity. His aspect, particularly in profile, had a strong character of acuteness and penetration.

In dress, he was a pattern of neatness and simplicity. A narrow, pleated stock, a coat with a small upright collar, no buckles at his knees, no silk or velvet in any part of his apparel, and a head as white as snow, gave an idea of something primitive and apostolical: while an air of neatness and cleanliness was diffused over his whole person — J. Hampson, *Memoirs of the late Rev. John Wesley*, 1791.

William Pitt, First Earl of Chatham (1708–1778)

English statesman, known as the 'Great Commoner'. Chief figure in coalition government; architect of military defeat of French in India and Canada. Set course of British Empire-building.

Pitt, it was expected, would take advantage of illness, and not appear [i.e. at the parliamentary enquiries into the loss of Minorca, 1757]. But he refined on that old finesse; and pretending to waive the care of a broken constitution, when his country demanded his service, and as a pledge of his sincerity in the scrutiny, he came to the discussion in all the studied apparatus of the valetudinarian. The weather was unseasonably warm; yet he was dressed in an old coat and waistcoat of beaver laced with gold; over this, a red surtout, the right arm lined with fur, and appendent with many black ribands, to indicate his inability of drawing it over his right arm, which hung in a crape sling, but which, in the warmth of speaking, he drew out with unlucky activity, and brandished as usual.

Pitt was undoubtedly one of the greatest masters of ornamental eloquence. His language was amazingly fine and flowing; his voice admirable; his action most expressive; his figure genteel and commanding. . . . Out of the House of Commons he was far from being this shining character. His conversation was affected and unnatural, his manner not engaging, nor his talents adapted to a country where Ministers must court, if they would be courted — Horace Walpole, *Memoirs*.

20 Historic Events

The Effect of the Union

The change of manners in the new generation was very remarkable. The Union with England carried many of our nobility and gentry to London. Sixty of the most considerable people [Members of Parliament] being obliged to pass half of the year there would no doubt change their Ideas. Besides, many English came to reside at Edinr. The Court of Exchaquer and the Bourds of Customs and Excise were mostly all of that nation; at least all the under officers were. These were people of fashion, and were well received by the first people here. As this intercourse with the English opend our Eyes a little, so it gave us a liberty of Trade we had not before. From the Union many of our younger Sons became marchants and went abroad. It likewise became the fashion for our young men of fortune to Study for some years in Holland, after which to make a tour throw France. On their return home they brought to Scotland Franch politeness grafted on the self importance and dignity of their Fathers. May we not suppose it was at this time our nation acquired the Character of poverty and pride? — Elizabeth Mure, *Some Observations of the Change of Manners in My Own Time, 1700-1790.*

Bubble Companies

The following are some of the Bubble Companies, which, on 12th July, 1720, were declared to be illegal by the Lords Justices assembled in Privy Council and were accordingly abolished:

1. For building and rebuilding houses throughout all England. Capital £3,000,000.
2. For supplying the town of Deal with fresh water.
3. For making of iron and steel in Great Britain.
4. For improving the land in the county of Flint. Capital

£1,000,000.

  5. For trading in hair.

  6. For carrying on an undertaking of great advantage: but nobody to know what it is.

  7. For paving the streets of London. Capital £2,000,000.

  8. For furnishing funerals to any part of Great Britain.

  9. For insuring of horses. Capital £2,000,000.

  10. For a grand dispensary. Capital £3,000,000.

  11. For a wheel for perpetual motion. Capital £1,000,000.

  12. For insuring and increasing children's fortunes.

  13. For insuring to all masters and mistresses the losses they may sustain by servants. Capital £2,000,000.

  14. For the importation of timber from Wales. Capital £2,000,000.

  15. For the transmutation of quicksilver into a malleable fine metal.

  16. For buying and fitting out ships to suppress pirates.

  17. For erecting loan-offices for the assistance and encouragement of the industries. Capital £2,000,000.

  18. For improving the art of making soap.

  19. For extracting silver from lead.

Etc., etc.

South Sea Bubble Bursts

Go on vile Traders, glory in your Sins,
And grow profusely Rich, by Wicked Means . . .
Impoverish Thousands by some Publick Fraud,
And worship Interest as your only God;
Though you may gain in Time, a South Sea Coach,
And ride through London, loaded with Reproach,
Become a proud Director, and at last,
Be bound to render what you got so fast;
Perhaps be punish'd when your All is lost;
With Gallows, Pillory or Whipping-Post,
Or if you have your Gold, be doom'd to float,
To Hell, in this infernal Ferry-boat.

The Weekly Journal or British Gazette, 13 May 1721.

The State of Scotland in 1724

August, 1724. Ther is a profound peace at present, and nothing stirring of any publick nature almost. Things are in suspense abroad, and, though our partys are warm enough in privat, and the humor great, yet there is little appearing in publick. Under this peace we are grouing much worse. The gentry and nobility are generally either discontent, or Jacobite, or profane; and the people are turning loose, worldly, and very disaffected. The poverty and debts of many are increasing, and I can not see hou it can be otherwise. Ther are no ways to bring in specie into this country. Trade is much failed, and any trade we have is of that kind that takes money from amongst us, and brings in French brandy, Irish meal, tea, etc. which are all consumed; and unles it be a feu coals from the West, and some black cattell from the South, and many of these are not our breed, but Irish, I see no branch of our business that brings in any money. Our tobacco trade, and other branches to the West Indies, are much sinking; and the prodigiouse run of our nobility and gentry to England, their wintering there, and educating their children there . . . takes away a vast deal of monney every year. Besides, it's plain that we are overstocked with people, considering their idlness, and that makes the consumpt very great. . . . To say nothing of the vast losses many have susteaned by the South Sea and York Building, our oun Fishing Company, which, wer people faithfull, might bring in a great deal, and other bubles — Robert Wodrow, *Analecta*.

The Story of Jenkins's Ear

Extract of the Narrative of Rob. Jenkins, *Master of the* Rebecca. — We sailed from Jamaica, with sugar, &c. for London; but Ap. 9. near the Havanna, a Spanish Guarde Costa came up, rowing with 16 oars, and firing several shot, order'd our boat to be sent on board her; in which went the Mate, with our clearance from Jamaica. They detained our men, and sent the boat back full of armed men, who told Cap. Jenkins, that they were come to visit his ship for money, logwood, &c. the product of the Spanish settlements. The Capt. answered, The King of Spain's Officers were wellcome; but that there was nothing on board, but what was the produce of Jamaica. Their number amounted to about 50 men: who broke open all her Hatches, lockers, and chests, but found nothing. Then their Lieutenant ordered Capt. Jenkins hands to be tied, and his Mates, and seized them to the fore-mast. Then they cut and violently beat a Mulatto boy: who confessing nothing, they put a rope about his neck, and another about the Captain's, which fastening together, they hoisted them up to the fore-yard: the boy slipt through the noose; and after a short space, they let the Capt. fall down amain on the deck, and asked him, if he would confess where his money was. He told them he had none; on which he was hoisted a second time, and swiftly let down again, and gave them the same answer. In about half an hour, one of them search'd his pockets, took his silver buckles out of his shoes; and then he was hoisted up again, and kept hanging 'till he was quite strangled; after which they let him fall down the fore-hatch upon the casks, which bruised him very much; from whence he was dragged by the neck upon the deck, where he lay to appearance dead for near a quarter of an hour. When he recover'd, their Lieutenant, with pistols and a cutlass, went to him, crying, Confess or die; he told him he had no more money than he shew'd him at first, being 4 guineas, 1 pistole, and 4 double doubloons; which being commanded, he gave him. No sooner had he done this, but the Lieut. took hold of his left ear, and with his cutlass slit it down; and another took hold of it and tore it off, but gave him the piece, bidding him carry it to his Majesty King George. His Mate and Boatswain were beat: the whole crew were stript of their cloaths, beds, &c. the Captain's own loss amounted to I 12s. They took away all his instruments of navigation, and all his candles. Being dismissed, the Capt. bore away for the Havannah: but those in the sloop stood after him, declaring that if he did not go immediately for the Gulph, they would set the ship on fire: and so rather than have a second visit from them, they recommended themselves to God; and after many great perils happily arrived in the Thames last friday. 4 *Ev.* – *The Story of Jenkins's Ear. From 'The Grub-street Journal' of 24 June 1731.*

The Black Hole of Calcutta, 21 June 1756

Figure to yourself, my friend, if possible, the situation of a hundred and forty-six wretches, exhausted by continual fatigue and action, crammed together in a cube of eighteen feet, in a close sultry night, in Bengal, shut up to the eastward and southward (the only quarters from whence air could reach us) by dead walls, and by a wall and door to the north, open only to the westward by two windows, strongly barred with iron, from which we could receive scarce any the least circulation of fresh air.

What must ensue, appeared to me in lively and dreadful colours, the instant I cast my eyes round and saw the size and situation of the room. Many unsuccessful attempts were made to force the door; for having nothing but our hands to work with, and the door opening inwards, all endeavours were vain and fruitless. . . .

We had been but few minutes confined before every one fell into a perspiration so profuse, you can form no idea of it. This brought on a raging thirst, which increased in proportion as the body was drained of its moisture.

. . . Before nine o'clock every man's thirst grew intolerable, and respiration difficult. Efforts were made again to force the door but in vain. Many insults were used to the guard to provoke them to fire in upon us. For my own part, I hitherto felt little pain or uneasiness, but what resulted from my anxiety for the sufferings of those within. By keeping my face between two of the bars, I obtained enough air to give my lungs easy play, though my perspiration was excessive and my thirst commencing.

Now everybody, excepting those situated in and near the windows, began to grow outrageous, and many delirious: 'Water, Water,' became the general cry. And the old Jemmautdaar [one of the guards outside the windows] . . . , taking pity on us, ordered the people to bring some skins of water. This was what I dreaded. I foresaw it would prove the ruin of the small chance left us, and essayed many times to speak to him privately to forbid its being brought; but the clamour was so loud, it became impossible. The water appeared. Words cannot paint to you the universal agitation and raving the sight of it threw us into. . . .

We had no means of conveying it into the prison, but by hats forced through the bars; and thus myself and Messieurs Coles and Scott . . . supplied them as fast as possible. But those who have experienced intense thirst . . . will be sufficiently sensible it could receive no more than a momentary alleviation; the cause still subsisted. Though we brought full hats within the bars, there ensued such violent struggles, and frequent contests to get at it, that before it reached the lips of any one, there would be scarcely a small tea cup left in them. These supplies like sprinkling water on fire, only served to feed and rouse the flame. . . .
The confusion now became general and horrid. Several quitted the other window (the only chance they had for life) to force their way to

the water, and the throng and press upon the window was beyond bearing; many forcing their passage from the further part of the room, pressed down those in their way, who had less strength, and trampled them to death.

From about nine to near eleven, I sustained this cruel scene and painful situation, still supplying them with water, though my legs were almost broke with the weight against them. By this time I myself was near pressed to death, and my two companions, with Mr. William Parker (who had forced himself into the window) were really so. . . .

For a great while they preserved a respect and regard to me, more than indeed I could expect, . . . but now all distinction was lost. My friend Baillie . . . and several others . . . had for some time been dead at my feet: and were now trampled upon by every corporal or common soldier, who, by the help of more robust constitutions, had forced their way to the window, and held fast by the bars over me, till at last I became so pressed and wedged up, I was deprived of all motion.

Determined now to give everything up, I called to them, and begged, as the last instance of their regard, they would remove the pressure upon me, and permit me to retire out of the window to die in quiet. They gave way; and with much difficulty I forced a passage into the centre of the prison, where the throng was less by the many dead (then I believe amounting to one third) and the numbers who flocked to the windows. . . .

In the black-hole there is a platform. . . . I travelled over the dead and repaired to the further end of it, just opposite to the other window. Here my poor friend Mr. Edward Eyre came staggering over the dead to me, and with his usual coolness and good nature, asked me how I did? but fell and expired before I had time to make him a reply. I laid myself down on some of the dead behind me, on the platform; and, recommending myself to heaven, had the comfort of thinking my sufferings could have no long duration.

My thirst grew now insupportable, and the difficulty of breathing much increased; and I had not remained in this situation I believe, ten minutes, when I was seized with a pain in my breast, and palpitation of heart. . . . These roused and obliged me to get up again. . . . I instantly determined to push for the window opposite to me, and . . . gained the third rank at it, with one hand seized a bar, and by that means gained the second. . . .

In a few moments the pain, palpitation, and difficulty of breathing ceased; but my thirst continued intolerable. I called aloud for 'Water for God's sake.' But from the water I had no relief; my thirst was rather' increased by it; so I determined to drink no more but patiently wait the event; and kept my mouth moist from time to time by sucking the perspiration out of my shirt-sleeves, and catching the drops as they fell, like heavy rain, from my head and face; you can hardly imagine how unhappy I was if any of them escaped my mouth. . . .

By half an hour past eleven, the much greater number of those living were in an outrageous delirium, and the others quite ungovernable; few retaining any calmness, but the ranks next the window. . . . They whose strength was exhausted, laid themselves down and expired quietly upon their fellows: others who had yet some strength and vigour left, made a last effort for the windows, and several succeeded by leaping and scrambling over the backs and heads of those in the first ranks: and got hold of the bars, from which there was no removing them. Many to the right and left sunk with the violent pressure, and were soon suffocated; for now a steam arose from the living and the dead. . . .

I was at this time sensible of no pain, and little uneasiness. I found a stupor coming on apace, and laid myself down by that gallant old man, the reverend Mr. Jervas Bellamy, who lay dead with his son the Lieutenant, hand in hand, near the southernmost wall of the prison.

When I had lain there some little time, I still had reflexion enough to suffer some uneasiness in the thought that I should be trampled upon when dead. . . . With some difficulty I raised myself and gained the platform a second time, where I presently lost all sensation. Of what passed in this interval to the time of my resurrection from this hole of horrors, I can give you no account.

When the day broke, and the gentlemen found that no entreaties could prevail to get the door opened, it occurred to one of them (I think to Mr. Secretary Cooke) to make a search for me, in hopes I might have influence enough to gain a release from this scene of misery. Accordingly Messrs. Lushington and Walcot undertook the search, and by my shirt discovered me under the dead upon the platform. They took me from thence and imagining I had some signs of life, brought me towards the window I had first possession of.

But as life was equally dear to every man (and the stench arising from the dead bodies was grown so intolerable), no one would give up his station in or near the window: so they were obliged to carry me back again. But soon after Captain Mills . . . who was in possession of a seat in the window, had the humanity to offer to resign it. I was again brought by the same gentlemen and placed in the window. At this juncture the *suba*, who had received an account of the havoc death had made amongst us, sent one of his Jemmautdaars to enquire if the chief survived. They showed me to him; told I had appearance of life remaining; and believed I might recover if the door was opened very soon. This answer being returned to the *suba*, an order came immediately for our release, it being then near six in the morning.

As the door opened inwards, and as the dead were piled up against it, and covered all the rest of the floor, it was impossible to open it by any efforts from without; it was therefore necessary that the dead should be removed by the few that were within, who were become so feeble, that the task, though it was the condition of life, was not performed without the utmost difficulty, and it was 20 minutes after the order came before the door could be opened.

About a quarter after six in the morning, the poor remains of 146 souls, being no more than three and twenty, came out of the Blackhole alive, but in a condition which made it very doubtful whether they would see the morning of the next day.... The bodies were dragged out of the hole by the soldiers, and thrown promiscuously into the ditch of an unfinished ravelin, which was afterwards filled with earth.... Mr. Holwell, when he came out of the prison was in a high fever, and not able to stand; he was, however, sent for to be examined by the viceroy, and was in this condition carried to his presence. It was some time before he could speak, but as soon as he was able, he began to relate the sufferings and death of his unhappy companions.

The viceroy, without taking any notice of this tale of distress, stopped him short, by telling him, that he had been informed there was treasure to a very considerable value secreted in the fort, and that if he did not discover it, he must expect no mercy. Mr. Holwell replied, that he knew of no such treasure; and then began to remind him of his assurance the day before, that no hurt should come either to himself or his friends. To this remonstrance he paid no more regard than he had done to the complaint, but proceeded in his enquiry concerning the treasure; and when he found no intelligence could be got, he ordered the general of his household troops, whose name was Mir Muddon, to take charge of Mr. Holwell as his prisoner.... Mr. Holwell and his associates in captivity, were conveyed in a kind of coach, drawn by oxen, called a hackney, to the camp, where they were loaded with fetters, and lodged in the tent of a Moorish soldier, which being no more than four feet by three feet, they were obliged to lie, sick as they were, half in and half out the whole night, which happened to be very rainy; yet the next day their fever happily came to a crisis, and boils broke out on every part of their bodies, which, though they were extremely painful, were the certain presages of their recovery. The next day they were removed to the coast, and, by order of General Mir Muddon, were soon after sent to sea by Maxadavad, the Metropolis of Bengal, to wait the viceroy's return, and be disposed of as he should farther determine.

At Maxadavad they arrived, after a voyage of thirteen days, in a huge boat, in which they had no better provision than rice and water, and no softer beds than some bamboos laid on the bottom timber of the vessel; they were, besides, exposed alternately to excessive heat and violent rains, without any covering, but a bit of old mat and some scraps of sacking. The boils that covered them were becoming running sores, and the irons on their legs had consumed the flesh almost to the bone.

When they arrived at Maxadavad, Mr. Holwell sent a letter to Mr. Law, the chief of the French factory, with an account of their distress, and Mr. Law, with great politeness and humanity, sent them not only clothes, linen, provision and liquors, in great plenty, but money — J.Z. Holwell's letter in the *Annual Register* for 1758.

Sir Hans Sloane and the Founding of the British Museum, 1759

'The immediate result of Sir Hans Sloane's death,' observed the uncle, 'was the foundation of the British Museum; for this great patron of science, being well aware how much it is benefited by the aggregation of various objects, and anxious that his fine collection should be preserved entire, directed by his will, that after his decease the whole of his Museum of natural and artificial curiosities, which had cost him £50,000, should be offered to Parliament for the moderate sum of £20,000, to be paid to his family.

'The contents of his collection were very various, and consisted of his library, books of drawings, MSS., &c., 50,000 volumes.

Medals and coins	. . .	23,000
Cameos, intaglios, seals, &c.		1,500

besides antique idols, anatomical preparations, amphibia, insects, minerals, volumes of dried plants, mathematical instruments, &c., the particulars of which were entered in a catalogue that was comprised in thirty-eight volumes folio, and eight volumes quarto.

21 Warfare

The Battle of Dettingen

Royal Welch Fusileers in action, 27 June 1743.

We attack'd the Regiment of *Navarre*, one of their prime regiments. Our People imitated their Predecessors in the last war gloriously, marching in close Order, as firm as a Wall, and did not fire till we came within 60 Paces, and still kept advancing; so that we had soon closed with the Enemy, if they had not retreated: For when the Smoak blew off a little, instead of being among their Living, we found the Dead in Heaps by us; and the second Fire turn'd them to the Right about, and upon a long Trot. We engaged two other Regiments afterwards, one

The Battle of Dettingen, 1743, in which George II (acting as Elector of Hanover) defeated the French army in Bavaria. This forced the French on the defensive and hastened successful negotiations with Savoy. Handel wrote a special *Te Deum* for the occasion.

after the other, who stood but one fire each; and their Blue *French* Foot Guards made the best of their Way without firing a Shot. Our Colonel fell in the first Attack, shot in the Mouth, and out at the Neck; but there are Hopes of his Recovery. The Gens d'Armes are quite ruin'd, who are their chief Dependance, and intended to cut us all to Pieces without firing a Shot. Our Regiment sustain'd little Loss, tho' much engaged; And indeed our whole Army gives us great Honour. Brigadier Huske who behaved gloriously, and quite cool was shot thro' the Foot at the Time that our Colonel fell, yet continued his Post. We have no more than 50 kill'd and wounded, and one Officer besides the Colonel. What preserved us, was our keeping close Order, and advancing near the Enemy ere we fir'd. Several that popp'd at 100 Paces lost more of their Men, and did less Execution; for the *French* will stand Fire at a distance, tho' 'tis plain they cannot look Men in the Face — *The Gentleman's Magazine*, 1743.

The Battle of Prestonpans, 21 September 1745

We began to march an hour before day, and happily for us, found no opposition, so that we had time to form before the enemy perceived us. The irregularity of the day before, or the difficulty of the passes, caused a general changement in the order of battle, for the Macdonalds who pretend it is due to them, took the right, though they were to have the left by lot, and the Camerons who were to have the right, had the left, but things did not go the worse for that changement, for every man did his duty, and no troops in the world could show more valour, than the Highlanders did that day. The Duke of Perth was at the right, and Lord George at the left; it was not yet day, so that we saw the enemy in good order of battle before they could see us; our dark clothes were advantageous to us.

As soon as they perceived us, their Cannon began to fire, but did little or no damage, and did not at all relent our march. Sullivan, who was at the right, seeing we had out-winged the enemy, cried out, 'Let the Macdonalds come to this hedge, we have out-winged them'; the Dragoons hearing this made a motion, as if they would extend themselves; upon which Sullivans cried out again, 'Let the first rank fire,' which they did; the Dragoons answered by a very irregular discharge, and went off, as fast as they could drive, and the Macdonalds after them, as fast as they; the foot finding themselves abandoned by the horse, flinched immediately after, so that there was a general deroute, and never such a one I believe in any action. The left, composed of the Camerons, Stewards of Appen and the Duke of Perth's Regiment which were almost all MacGregors, behaved most gloriously, for they rushed in with such fury upon the enemy, after their first discharge, that they had not time to charge their cannon, and then the broadswords played their part, for with one stroke, arms, and legs were cut off, and heads were split to the shoulders, never such wounds were seen. Cope escaped with the few that followed him by the breaches that he caused to be made in those stone walls near Gardener's House and it was there really where the great slaughter was, for the poor soldiers that could not pass in those breaches because of the Dragoons that filled them up, were cut to pieces, and the Dragoons themselves were pursued so closely . . . that they were obliged to abandon their horses and throw themselves into those parks where the most of them were taken. The Dragoons, in their flight, threw away their Standards, the foot their Colours; one found in one place, another in another, but the the people of the country took away a great many of them, there were eighty-four officers made prisoners, of all ranks and about fourteen hundred private men. . . .

. . . But when people began to be cool, they reflected on the danger the Prince exposed himself to, notwithstanding what he had promised. . . . The Prince answered that he was obliged to them all, for the care and tenderness they had of him, that he only did what he ought to do, and that he would never forget their behaviour that day. They then proposed him to refresh and repose himself, that he had great need of it; 'No,' says he, with a tender heart and in a most feeling way, 'I can't rest until I see my own poor men taken care of, and the other wounded too, for they are the King's subjects as well as we, and it's none of their fault if they are led on blindly', upon which he immediately sent orders, to the neighbouring villages, upon pain of military execution that houses and everything necessary should be provided for the wounded, and that the inhabitants should come with spades and other instruments to bury the dead. He spoke to the surgeons, first to dress the Highlanders, and afterwards to neglect nothing for the others; he neither would eat or drink until he saw people set about this – John William O'Sullivan in A. and H. Tayler, *The 1745 and After.*

The Disaster of Culloden, 1746

From the inequality of this marsh ground, our right and centre came first up with the enemy, our first line advancing a little obliquely; but, overpowered by a murderous fire in front and flank, our right could not maintain its ground and was obliged to give way, whilst our centre had already broken the enemy's first line and attacked the second. The left wing, where I was with Scothouse, was not twenty paces from the enemy, who gave their first fire at the moment the flight began to become general, which spread from the right to the left of our army with the rapidity of lightning. What a spectacle of horror! The same Highlanders, who had advanced to the charge like lions, with bold, determined countenances, were in an instant seen flying like trembling cowards in the greatest disorder. It may be said of the attack of the Highlanders, that it bears great resemblance to that of the French; that it is a flame, the violence of which is more to be dreaded than the duration. No troops, however excellent, are possessed of qualities which will render them constantly invincible.

It was evident our destruction would become inevitable, if the English got possession of the enclosure. The Prince saw this from the eminence where he was posted, and sent his aide-de-camp six or seven times, ordering Lord George to take possession of it. He saw that his orders were not executed, but yet he never quitted his place on the eminence. This was a critical moment when he ought to have displayed the courage of a grenadier, by immediately advancing to put himself at the head of his army, and commanding himself those manoeuvres which he wished to be executed. He would never have experienced disobedience on the part of his subjects who had exposed their lives and fortunes to establish him on the throne of his ancestors, and who would have shed for him the last drop of their blood. There are occasions when a general ought to expose his person, and not remain beyond the reach of musketry, and surely there never was a more pressing occasion for disregarding a few shots than the one in question, as the gain or loss of the battle depended on it. In the desperate expedition on which he had entered, though it was proper that he should guard against danger, he ought to have done so in a manner which showed that life or death was equally indifferent to him, conducting himself with valour and prudence, according to circumstances. But he was surrounded by Irish confidants, whose baseness of soul corresponded to the obscurity of their birth. The natives of Ireland are generally supposed, in England, to have a great confusion of ideas, and they are in general very bad counsellors. But the Prince blindly adopted their opinions.

As far as I could distinguish, at the distance of twenty paces, the English appeared to be drawn up in six ranks, the three first being on their knees, and keeping up a terrible running fire on us. My unfortunate friend Scothouse was killed by my side, but I was not so deeply affected at the moment of his fall as I have been ever since. It would almost seem as if the Power that presides over the lives of men in battles marks out the most deserving for destruction and spares those who are more unworthy. Military men, susceptible of friendship, are much to be pitied. The melancholy fate of my friends has often cost me many a tear, and left on my heart an indelible impression of pain and regret. Mr Macdonald of Keppoch, who had been absent on leave with his clan, having made great haste to join the Prince, arrived at the moment of the charge, in time to take his station in the first line with his clan, where he was instantly killed. He was a gentleman of uncommon merit, and his death was universally lamented – the Chevalier de Johnstone, *A Memoir of the 'Forty-Five, c.* 1820.

The Battle of Colloden, 1746, near Inverness, in which the Duke of Cumberland defeated the forces of the Young Pretender.

News of Culloden Reaches London

I was in the coffeehouse with Smollett when the news of the battle of Culloden arrived, and when London all over was in a perfect uproar of joy.... About 9 o'clock I wished to go home to Lyon's, in New Bond Street, as I had promised to sup with him that night, it being the anniversary of his marriage night, or the birthday of one of his children. I asked Smollett if he was ready to go, as he lived at Mayfair; he said he was, and would conduct me. The mob were so riotous, and the squibs so numerous and incessant that we were glad to go into a narrow entry to put our wigs in our pockets, and to take our swords from our belts and walk with them in our hands, as everybody then wore swords; and, after cautioning me against speaking a word, lest the mob should discover my country and become insolent, 'for John Bull,' says he, 'is as haughty and valiant to-night as he was abject and cowardly on the Black Wednesday when the Highlanders were at Derby.'... Smollett, though a Tory, was not a Jacobite, but he had the feelings of a Scotch gentleman on the reported cruelties that were said to be exercised after the battle of Culloden – Alexander Carlyle, *Autobiography*, 1746.

The Highlands after the 'Forty-Five

The last rebellion, however, gave occasion to memorable changes of every kind. Many chieftains lost their lives either in the field or on the scaffold, or were forced into exile, and their estates forfeited. The whole weight of Government, for a number of years, was employed to dissolve every tie between the chief and the clan, and to abolish all distinctions between the Highland and Lowland Scots. Even the gentry who had not been engaged in the rebellion, found it expedient to drop some of their national customs, which either gave offence, or were prohibited by law. It was doubtless with reluctance that people advanced in life complied with these innovations. But these old-fashioned gentlemen being now mostly gone, their successors have no longer the same attachment either to their people or to ancient modes of life. They affect the manners of the Lowland gentry, but in general they retain their hospitality and courtesy to strangers, especially those that come properly recommended.

The middling and inferior classes of Highlanders, who have been little out of their own country, retain the domestic manners of their forefathers in great purity. In the remote countries, apart from military roads, the traveller will meet with hospitality worthy of the patriarchal or heroic times. . . . An old tenant told me once with great simplicity, that he allowed nobody to pass his house without bread and cheese and a drink of milk or whey; but if a gentleman or minister came into the glen, he killed a lamb or a kid — John Ramsay, *Scotland and Scotsmen in the Eighteenth Century*.

Threat of Invasion by the French Flat-Bottomed Boats at Dunkirk, 1755

When the newspapers swarm with our military preparations at home, with encampments, fire-ships, floating castles at the mouths of the great rivers, etc, in short, when we expect an invasion, you would chide, or be disposed to chide me, if I were quite silent — and yet, what can I tell you more than that an invastion is threatened, that sixteen thousand men are about Dunkirk, and that they are assembling great quantities of flat-bottomed boats! . . . You will ask me, if we are alarmed? the people not at all so: a minister or two, who are subject to alarms, and — and that is no bad circumstance. We are as much an island as ever, and I think a much less exposed one than we have been for many years. Our fleet is vast; our army at home, and ready, and two-thirds stronger than when we were threatened in 1744: the season has been the wettest that ever has been known, consequently the roads not very invadeable. . . . We are a comical nation (I speak with all due regard to our gravity!) — it were a pity we should be destroyed, if it were only for the sake of posterity; we shall not be half so droll, if we were either a province to France, or under an absolute prince of our own — Horace Walpole.

The Battle of Plassey, 23 June 1757

I gave you an account of the taking of Chandernagore; the subject of this address is an event of much higher importance, no less than the entire overthrow of Nabob Suraj-ud-Daulah, and the placing of Meer

Jaffier on the throne. I intimated in my last how dilatory Suraj-ud-Daulah appeared in fulfilling the articles of the treaty. This disposition not only continued but increased, and we discovered that he was designing our ruin by a conjunction with the French. To this end Monsieur Bussy was pressingly invited to come into this province, and Monsieur Law of Cossimbazar was ordered to return from Patna.

About this time some of his principal officers made overtures to us for dethroning him. At the head of these was Meer Jaffier, then Bukhshee to the army, a man as generally esteemed as the other was detested. As we had reason to believe this disaffection pretty general, we soon entered into engagements with Meer Jaffier to put the crown on his head. All necessary preparations being completed with the utmost secrecy, the army, consisting of about one thousand Europeans and two thousand sepoys, with eight pieces of cannon, marched from Chandernagore on the 13th and arrived on the 18th at Cutwa Fort. The 22nd, in the evening, we crossed the river, and landing on the island, marched straight for Plassey Grove, where we arrived by one in the morning.

At daybreak we discovered the Nabob's army moving towards us, consisting, as we since found, of about fifteen thousand horse and thirty-five thousand foot, with upwards of forty pieces of cannon. They approached apace, and by six began to attack with a number of heavy cannon, supported by the whole army, and continued to play on us very briskly for several hours, during which our situation was of the utmost service to us, being lodged in a large grove with good mud banks. To succeed in an attempt on their cannon was next to impossible, as they were planted in a manner round us, and at considerable distances from each other. We therefore remained quiet in our post, in expectation of a successful attack upon their camp at night.

About noon the enemy drew off their artillery, and retired to their camp.... We immediately sent a detachment accompanied with two field-pieces, to take possession of a tank with high banks, which was advanced about three hundred yards above our grove, and from which the enemy had considerably annoyed us with some cannon managed by Frenchmen. This motion brought them out a second time; but on finding them make no great effort to dislodge us, we proceeded to take possession of one or two more eminences lying very near an angle of their camp.... They made several attempts to bring out their cannon, but our advance field-pieces played so warmly and so well upon them that they were always drove back. Their horse exposing themselves a good deal on this occasion, many of them were killed, and among

Robert Clive, 1725-74, by Sir Nathaniel Dance-Holland. Clive was a British soldier and administrator. Serving the East India Company he won a series of victories, notably Calcutta and Plassey, 1757, consolidating British power and ousting the French. As Governor of Bengal he promoted reform.

the rest four or five officers of the first distinction, by which the whole army being visibly dispirited and thrown into some confusion, we were encouraged to storm both the eminence and the angle of their camp, which were carried at the same instant, with little or no loss. . . . On this a general rout ensued; and we pursued the enemy six miles, passing upwards of forty pieces of cannon they had abandoned, with an in-

163

finite number of carriages filled with baggage of all kinds. Suraj-ud-Daulah escaped on a camel, and reaching Moorshedabad early next morning, despatched away what jewels and treasure he conveniently could, and he himself followed at midnight with only two or three attendants.

It is computed there are killed of the enemy about five hundred. Our loss amounted to only twenty-two killed and fifty wounded, and those chiefly blacks. During the warmest part of the action we observed a large body of troops hovering on our right, which proved to be our friends; but as they never discovered themselves by any signal whatsoever, we frequently fired on them to make them keep their distance. When the battle was over they sent a congratulatory message, and encamped in our neighbourhood that night. The next day Meer Jaffier paid me a visit, and expressed much gratitude at the service done him, assuring me in the most solemn manner that he would faithfully perform his engagement to the English — Robert Clive's letter to the Secret Committee of the Court of Directors of the East India Company: dated 26 July 1757.

The Battle of Quebec, 13 September 1759

Before day-break this morning we made a descent upon the north shore, about half a quarter of a mile to the eastward of Sillery; . . . we had, in this debarkation, thirty flat-bottomed boats, containing about sixteen hundred men. This was a great surprise on the enemy, who, from the natural strength of the place, did not suspect, and consequently were not prepared against, so bold an attempt. . . . As fast as we landed, the boats put off for reinforcements . . . the General, with Brigadiers, Monckton and Murray, were a-shore with the first division. We lost no time here, but clambered up one of the steepest precipices that can be conceived, being almost a perpendicular, and of an incredible height. As soon as we gained the summit, all was quiet, and not a shot was heard, owing to the excellent conduct of the light infantry under Colonel Howe; it was by this time clear day-light. Here we formed again . . . we then faced to the right, and marched towards the town by files, till we came to the plains of Abraham; an even piece of ground which Mr. Wolfe had made choice of, while we stood forming upon the hill. Weather showery: about six o'clock the enemy made their appearance upon the heights, between us and the town; whereupon we halted, and wheeled to the right, thereby forming the line of battle. . . . The enemy had now likewise formed the line of battle, and got some cannon to play on us, with round and canister shot; but what galled us most was a body of Indians and other marksmen they had concealed in the corn opposite to the front of our right wing . . . but Colonel Hale . . . advanced some platoons . . . which, after a few rounds, obliged these skulkers to retire. We were now ordered to lie down, and remained some time in this position. About eight o'clock we had two pieces of short brass six-pounders playing on the enemy, which threw them into some confusion. . . . About ten o'clock the enemy began to advance briskly in three columns, with loud shouts and recovered arms, two of them inclining to the left of our army, and the third towards our right, firing obliquely at the two extremities of our line, from the distance of one hundred and thirty, until they came within forty yards; which our troops withstood with the greatest intrepidity and firmness, still reserving their fire, and paying the strictest obedience to their Officers: this uncommon steadiness, together with the havoc which the grape-shot from our field-pieces made among them, threw them into some disorder, and was most critically maintained by a well-timed, regular and heavy discharge of our small arms, such as they could no longer oppose; hereupon they gave way, and fled with precipitation, so that, by the time the cloud of smoke was vanished, our men were again loaded, and profiting by the advantage we had over them, pursued them almost to the gates of the town, and the bridge over the little river, redoubling our fire with great eagerness, making many Officers and men prisoners. The weather cleared up, with a comfortably warm sunshine. . . . Our joy at this success is inexpressibly damped by the loss we sustained of one of the greatest heroes which this or any other age can boast of — General James Wolfe, who received his mortal wound as he was exerting himself at the head of the grenadiers of Louisbourg. . . . The officers who are prisoners say that Quebec will surrender in a few days: some deserters, who came out to us in the evening, agree in that opinion, and inform us, that the Sieur de Montcalm is dying, in great agony, of a wound he received today in their retreat. . . .

After our late worthy general, of renowned memory, was carried off wounded, to the rear of the front line, he desired those who were about him to lay him down; being asked if he would have a Surgeon, he replied, 'It is needless; it is all over with me'. One of them then cried out, 'They run, see how they run'. 'Who runs?' demanded our hero, with great earnestness, like a person roused from sleep. The

From the French, General James Wolfe captures Quebec, the key to Canada, 13 September 1759. From a contemporary engraving.

Officer answered, 'The enemy, Sir, Egad they give way everywhere'.
Thereupon the General rejoined, 'Go one of you, my lads, to Colonel
Burton; tell him to march Webb's regiment with all speed down to
Charles's river, to cut off the retreat of the fugitives from the bridge'.
Then, turning to his side, he added, 'Now; God be praised, I will die
in peace:' and thus expired – *Journal of Captain John Knox.*

22 England and the Sea

Admiral Vernon at Cartagena

Princess Caroline, in the harbour of
Cartagena, 31st March, 1741

My dear,

After the glorious success it has pleased Almighty God so wonderfully to favour us with, Whose manifold mercies I hope I shall never be unmindful of, I cannot omit laying hold of the opportunity of an express I am sending home to acquaint you of the joyful news, though in my present hurries I have no leisure to enter into many particulars. . .

The first attack was by three of my 80-gun ships on the forts of St. Jago and St. Philip, lying without Boca Chica Castle, to secure a descent; and we drove the enemy out of them in less than an hour, and secured a descent to the army, and without their having so much as a single musket-shot fired at them. And my gallant sailors twice stormed and took two batteries on the opposite side of the harbour; the one of fifteen, the other of five 24-pounders, which the general complained of to me galled his army; they having remounted guns and repaired it after our first destroying it, as it lay well to play on our land battery.

On the propitious 25th March, the day I took charge, the General sent me word he intended to storm Boca Chica Castle; upon which, before the time he proposed, I sent all my boats manned and armed to land at those destroyed batteries a third time, for making a diversion on that side, to favour their storming it. But the enemy was under such consternation, that our troops marched into the castle over the breach without having a single shot fired at them, and about ten at night my gallant sailors stormed at St. Joseph's fort without the ceremony of a breach, from whence, all the first of the night, the enemy had been firing partridge-shot at our men through the bushes, but with little injury to them; but they would not stand the assault, but deserted the fort, leaving only three drunken Spaniards behind them. Flushed with this success, my officers finding the Spaniards burning and sinking their ships, part of the boats were detached, to try what could be saved; and they boarded and took the Spanish admiral's ship, the *Gallicia*, with the flag flying, and in her the captain of the ship, the captain of the marines, an ensign, and 60 men, who, not having boats to escape, gave us the opportunity of saving this ship, which they had orders to sink likewise. Besides the admiral's ship taken, of 70 guns, they burnt the *St. Philip*, of 80 guns, and sunk the *St. Carlos* and *Africa*, of 60 guns each, across the channel; and they have this day sunk the *Conquistador* and *Dragon*, of 60 guns each, the only remaining men-of-war here, as they have done all the galleons and other vessels lying above Castillo Grande near five leagues higher up the harbour.

I have only time to add, it has pleased Almighty God to preserve me in good health, to go through all these glorious fatigues, and in a full disposition to push this beginning with all possible vigour, to humble the proud Spaniards, and bring them to repentance for all the injuries and long-practised depredations on us.

I have only time to send you my sincerest love and affection for you and blessing to our dear boys; and with services to all our good neighbours, and honest Will Fisher,

I am, my dearest,

Your most affectionate husband,

E. Vernon

'Foulweather Jack' to the South Seas

The Honourable Mr. Byron, 'Foulweather Jack', later Vice Admiral, was the grandfather of Lord Byron, who left a reference to him in 'An Epistle to Augusta':

> *A strange doom is thy father's son's, and past*
> *Recalling, as it lies beyond redress.*
> *Reversed for him our grandsires' fate of yore,*
> *He had no rest on sea nor I on shore.*

Sunday the 18th Day of October, 1741, at Noon, the Cutter came off, and brought aboard Plenty of Shell-fish and Greens. The Honourable Mr. Byron, Mr. Campbell and three of the Barge's Crew, came from where the Barge lay. Mr. Byron came aboard, and inform'd us of the Barge's being safe in the Bay, where we left her, and only waited the Opportunity of Weather to come round with her: At the same Time he desired to know, if we would give him, and those who would stay with Captain Cheap, their Share of Provisions. This Question of Mr Byron's very much surpriz'd us; and what surpriz'd us more was, that he should be influenc'd by Mr Campbell, a Person whom he always held in Contempt. As for my Part, I believe Mr. Byron left us because he could not get any Accommodation aboard the Vessel that he lik'd, being oblig'd to lie forward with the Men; as were also the Carpenter and myself, when below: It is very certain, that we are so closely pent up for want of room, that the worst Jail in England is a Palace to our present Situation.

John Bulkeley and John Cummins, Gunner and Carpenter of
the *Wager, A Voyage to the South Seas*, 1740-1.

Instructions for Training from the Naval Academy in 1742

Whereas the bearer, Mr. William Lloyd, has been educated in the Naval Academy at Portsmouth, and is well qualified to serve his Majesty at sea, you are hereby required and directed to . . . enter him as one of your Complement.

You are to take care that he applies himself to the Duty of a Seaman, and he is to have the Privilege of walking the Quarter Deck. You are to allot him a proper place to lie in without setting up any cabin, and you are to rate him volunteer per order which will entitle him to Able-Seaman's pay.

You are to oblige him to keep a Journal, and to draw the appearances of Head-lands, Coasts, Bays, Sands, Rocks and Suchlike: and you are to take care that the Master, Boatswain and Schoolmaster do instruct him in all parts of learning that may qualify him to do the duty of Able Seaman and Midshipman.

After two years' Service at Sea you are to rate him Midshipman ordinary, or Midshipman if he shall be qualified for it.

When your Ship shall be at Spithead, or in Portsmouth Harbour, you are to direct him to attend the Mathematical Master in order to his further improvement in the Mathematicks, and likewise to attend the lessons given by the other teachers and by the officers of the yard, who are directed to instruct him Gratis.

He is likewise to carry his Journal to the Mathematical Master in order to his examining the same: and representing to us how he has informed himself. And at the end of his Service in the Ship under your

Command you are to give him such a Certificate of his Sobriety, Diligence and Skill in the Profession of a Seaman as he shall deserve, as also the length of Time he has served with you either as a Volunteer per order or Midshipman.

Life in the Navy

The great bulwark of this nation is our naval force; a bulwark which, if kept carefully repaired, is capable of excluding our enemies for ever; and, in truth, the only fortification by which we can be able to preserve that security which is the foundation of public happiness. This particular service, so necesssary to the very existence of this Government lies at present under sufficient hardships and disadvantages; let us take care how we subject it to any further or greater inconveniences, lest they should render the service insupportable to our sailors, which must end in the utter ruin of this country. . . . Our sailors are already, by the nature of their employment, exposed to difficulties which we cannot relieve, and to hardships which we cannot redress; they endure, by the defective constitution of improper conduct of our navy, many additional miseries, which I would contribute the utmost in my power to mitigate. It seems necessary, Sir, to take into our consideration the service of the sea, and to appoint a committee to inquire into the cause of the present navy debt, that we may at last understand the reason why the present sea tickets bear such an enormous discount, and why the poor sailors and their families are forced to take up their wages at the loss of above half the sum for which their notes are given. . . . This is, however, not the only nor the greatest hardship of our sailors; there are other corruptions that require to be stopped or defects which need to be supplied. Our fleets, which are defrauded by injustice, are first manned by violence and maintained by cruelty. When our ships are to be fitted, an impress is sent into the streets, to bring those who shall fall in the way, by force into the vessels; from that time they are, in effect, condemned to death; since they are never allowed to set foot again on shore, but turned over from ship to ship, and when they have finished one expedition, hurried into another, without any regard to the hardships they have undergone, or the length of the voyage; so that they must live upon salt provisions, without their pay, till they shall be consumed by the scurvy, or die of some other distemper, which they have contracted by the hardships they have suffered and the provisions on which they have been obliged to subsist: a practice so horrid and barbarous, that it is sufficient to deter anyone from entering into the service at all, and to oblige those who are so unfortunate as to be engaged in it, to desert to the enemy, or fall upon the most desperate means to set themselves free from such dreadful servitude. Nor can it easily be guessed why it has not provoked the sailors to some universal mutiny which might produce the utter ruin of this kingdom; a consequence which every day may be supposed to bring nearer, as the same cruelty grows perpetually more hateful by daily repetition.

Here is a grievance which cannot be mentioned without horror, or remain unredressed without the greatest danger and the most flagrant guilt. And, surely it is an inquiry well worthy of this assembly, whether the royal navy may not be supplied by milder methods; for if any more convenient way can be found, and we neglect to use it, we are guilty of no less than the murder of those poor wretches, besides the loss of their service and the danger of their revolt — Admiral Vernon, House of Commons, 1749.

Execution of Admiral Byng

On Monday, March 14th, 1757, all the men-of-war at Spithead were ordered to send their boats with the captains and all the officers of each ship, accompanied with a party of marines under arms, to attend the execution of Mr. Byng. Accordingly they rowed from Spithead, and made the harbour a little after 11 o'clock, with the utmost difficulty and danger, it blowing prodigiously hard at N.W. by N., and the tide of ebb against them. It was still more difficult to get up so high as the *Monarque* lay, on board which ship the admiral suffered. Notwithstanding it blew so hard and the sea ran very high, there was a prodigious number of other boats round the ship, on the outside of the ship's boats, which last kept all others off. Not a soul was suffered to be aboard the *Monarque*, except those belonging to the ship. Mr. Byng, accompanied by a clergyman who attended him during his confinement, and two gentlemen of his relations, about 12 came on the quarterdeck, when he threw his hat on the deck, kneeled on a cushion, tied a handkerchief over his eyes, and dropping another which he held in his hand as a signal, a volley from six marines was fired, five of whose bullets went through him, and he was no more. He died with great resolution and composure, not showing the least sign of timidity in the awful moment — *Naval History of Great Britain*, 1758.

The Battle of Quiberon Bay, 20 November 1759

Royal George, of Penris Point,
November 24th, 1759.

Sir,

In my letter of the 17th by express, I desired you would acquaint their Lordships with my having received intelligence of eighteen sail of the line, and three frigates of the Brest squadron being discovered about twenty-four leagues to the north-west of Belleisle, steering to the eastward. All the prisoners, however, agree that on the day we chased them, their squadron consisted, according to the accompanying list, of four ships of eighty, six of seventy-four, three of seventy, eight of sixty-four, one frigate of thirty-six, one of thirty-four, and one of sixteen guns, with a small vessel to look out. They sailed from Brest the 14th instant, the same day I sailed from Torbay. Concluding that their first rendevous would be Quiberon, the instant I received the intelligence I directed my course thither with a pressed sail. At first the wind blowing hard at S. b. E. and S. drove us considerably to the westward. But on the 18th and 19th, though variable, it proved more favourable. In the meantime having been joined by the *Maidstone* and *Coventry* frigates, I directed their commanders to keep ahead of the squadron, one on the starboard, and the other on the larboard bow. At half-past eight o'clock on the morning of the 20th, Belleisle, by our reckoning, bearing E. b. N. ¼ N. about thirteen leagues, the *Maidstone* made the signal for seeing a fleet. I immediately spread abroad the signal for the line abreast, in order to draw all the ships of the squadron up with me. I had before sent the *Magnanime* ahead to make the land. At three-quarters past nine she made the signal for seeing an enemy. Observing, on my discovering them, that they made off, I threw out the signal for the seven ships nearest them to chase, and draw into a line of battle ahead of me, and endeavour to stop them till the rest of the squadron should come up, who were also to form as they chased, that no time might be lost in the pursuit. . . . Monsieur Conflans kept going off under such sail as all his squadron could carry, and at the same time keep together; while we crowded after him with every sail our ships could bear. At half-past two p.m. the fire beginning ahead, I made the signal for engaging. We were then to the south-ward of Belleisle, and the French Admiral headmost, soon after led round

173

A detail of the Battle of Quiberon Bay, 20 November 1759. Admiral Hawke defeated decisively the French fleet under de Conflans. This ended plans of France for invading Britain.

the Cardinals, while his rear was in action. About four o'clock the *Formidable* struck, and a little after, the *Thésée* and *Superbe* were sunk. About five, the *Heros* struck, and came to an anchor, but it blowing hard, no boat could be sent to board her. Night was now come, and being on a part of the coast, among islands and shoals, of which we were totally ignorant, without a pilot, as was the greatest part of the squadron, and blowing hard on a lee shore, I made the signal to anchor, and come-to in fifteen-fathom water. . . . In the night we heard many guns of distress fired, but, blowing hard, want of knowledge of the coast, and whether they were fired by a friend or an enemy, prevented all means of relief. . . .

As soon as it was broad daylight, in the morning of the 21st, I discovered seven or eight of the enemy's line-of-battle ships at anchor between Point Penris and the river Vilaine, on which I made the signal to weigh in order to work up and attack them. But it blowed so hard from the N.W. that instead of daring to cast the squadron loose, I was obliged to strike topgallant masts. Most of the ships appeared to be aground at low water. . . .

In attacking a flying enemy, it was impossible in the space of a short winter's day that all our ships should be able to get into action, or all those of the enemy brought to it. The commanders and companies of such as did come up with the rear of the French on the 20th behaved with the greatest intrepidity, and gave the strongest proofs of a true British spirit. In the same manner I am satisfied would those have acquitted themselves whose bad-going ships, or the distance they were at in the morning, prevented from getting up.

Our loss by the enemy is not considerable. For in the ships which are now with me, I find only one lieutenant and fifty seamen and marines killed, and about two hundred and twenty wounded.

When I consider the season of the year, the hard gales on the day of action, a flying enemy, the shortness of the day, and the coast they were on, I can boldly affirm that all that could possibly be done has been done. As to the loss we have sustained, let it be placed to the account of the necessity I was under of running all risks to break this strong force of the enemy. Had we had but two hours more daylight, the whole had been totally destroyed or taken; for we were almost up with their van when night overtook us. . . .

> I am, etc.,
> Edward Hawke.
> Letter from Admiral Sir Edward Hawke